NEW FORMS OF
WORK ORGANIZATION

NEW FORMS
OF WORK
ORGANIZATION:

The Challenge for North American Unions

TOM RANKIN

University of Toronto Press

Toronto   Buffalo   London

© University of Toronto Press 1990
Toronto Buffalo London
Printed in Canada

ISBN 0-8020-2698-2

Printed on acid-free paper.

Canadian Cataloguing in Publication Data

Rankin, Thomas Donald
   New forms of work organization: The challenge for North American unions

   Includes bibliographical references.
   ISBN 0-8020-2698-2

   1. Energy and Chemical Workers Union. Local 800.
   2. Shell Canada Products Limited.
   3. Trade unions – Ontario – Sarnia – Case studies.
   4. Industrial relations – Ontario – Sarnia – Case studies.
   5. Work – Case studies.   I. Title.

HD6528.C452E6 1990   331.88′16′00971327   C90-094196-0

This book has been published with the help of
a grant from the Social Science Federation of
Canada, using funds provided by the Social
Sciences and Humanities Research Council of
Canada.

65 088

For Jesse and Zachary

Contents

ACKNOWLEDGMENTS ix

PREFACE xi

1 Industrial Unionism and the Legacy of Scientific
Management 3

2 New Forms of Work Organization and the Union
Response 41

3 The Shell Sarnia Chemical Plant: The Future
in the Present? 60

4 The Chemical Plant Collective Bargaining System 76

5 ECWU Local 800: Beyond Industrial Unionism 116

6 Concluding Remarks 147

APPENDICES
I Collective Agreement between Shell Canada
Products Limited and the Energy and Chemical
Workers Union Local 800 157
II Good Work Practices Handbook 163
III Sarnia Chemical Plant Philosophy Statement
Related to Work Design 165

NOTES 169

BIBLIOGRAPHY 173

INDEX 189

Acknowledgments

I am deeply indebted to my colleague, Jacquie Mansell, who has been an invaluable source of advice and learning throughout the four years it has taken to complete this book.

I also wish to thank Eleanor Dudar, Björn Gustavsen, Norm Halpern, Larry Hirschhorn, Harvey Koldnoy, Wayne Roberts, Åke Sandberg, Eric Trist, and Hans van Beinum for their advice and encouragement and the management of Shell Canada for their co-operation and valuable perspective.

Finally, I wish to thank the members and officials of ECWU local 800, in particular Judy McKibbon and Stu Sullivan. This book would not have been possible without their collective co-operation, competence, and courage.

Preface

The decline of Taylorism throughout the western industrialized world and the subsequent development of new forms of work organization have been accompanied by considerable controversy and debate. Especially in Canada and the United States, few issues have stirred emotions as has the relation between unions and these new forms. For some, quality of working life (QWL), employee involvement (EI), Japanese manufacturing practices, etc., in an almost apolitical way make unions redundant. According to this line of reasoning unions are a consequence of 'bad' management – improve management and you eliminate the need for unions. For others, these few forms are integral components of conscious managerial strategies to update capital's control of the labour process. Limited worker involvement in shop/office-floor issues and token union participation in management decisions endow workers and unions with a false consciousness of their real interests. For still others, these new forms signal the birth of a new era of co-operation in labour-management relations. In this view, the traditional adversarial relationship is dismissed as an anachronism, an unfortunate legacy of the quickly receding industrial past, out of step with the needs of the emerging social, technological, and economic order. Part and parcel of this new order is a new unionism, one which strives to integrate its goals with those of its management partner. Finally, there are those who argue that these new forms offer unions the possibility to revitalize their ongoing struggle to democratize not only the workplace but society at large.

Underlying all but the last of these views is the fear that new forms of work organization spell the end of anything resembling a strong, independent union movement. Especially in the United States, this would appear to be a real possibility. But Canadian unions have little cause for complacency. Even in Sweden, home of the strongest union movement in the western world, the question 'Can Swedish unions live without Taylor?' (Von Otter 1987) is asked only partly in jest. In grappling with the possibility of such a dismal future unions can adopt several positions. One is to ignore the new work forms in the belief that, like many organization innovations, they are in fact insignificant and will soon fade away. More and more evidence, however, suggests this is not the case. To oversimplify, new forms of work organization change for management and labour not only the rules of the game but the game itself. To use Sandberg's (1987) formulation, the game is changing from one of 'distribution' to one of 'production.' Traditionally unions had assumed, as had Galbraith (1958), that the problem of production had been solved. Accordingly, the work of unions has been directed primarily at influencing the distribution of the results of production (of both goods and services). Distribution issues will remain critical in the future; indeed distribution and production issues cannot be separated. However, the emerging 'terrain of contest' between labour and management is being shaped fundamentally by issues of production. For unions to decline from actively participating in this change would be to run the risk of being reduced to the role of spectator to what may prove to be a more important change in the workplace than the introduction of the microprocessor.

A second position is to resist the introduction of these new forms of organization. From a pure balance-of-power perspective, vis-à-vis management, this is simply not possible. Moreover, such a position would put union leaders at odds not only with history but as well with much of their membership who value or will value the real opportunities for skill development and meaningful work provided by these changes in work organization. As Mansell (1987b) puts it, workers may find new-style management more appealing than old-style unionism.

The challenge for unions is to seize the opportunity to influence working life as Taylorism gives way to a new pattern of values, concepts, and techniques about work organization. Both the period of transition and the post-Taylorist pattern will be much more fluid and open than their predecessors. Any period of significant change not only allows but demands considerable experimentation before 'successful' models emerge. Furthermore, it is questionable whether any *one* such model will ever emerge. More likely, we are entering a phase where the capacity to generate models continuously will be the central issue in how work is organized (Gustavsen 1985). There is space, therefore, for unions to develop a strategic rather than just a reactive response to new forms of work organization.

Is such a strategy possible or will some version of the non-union future come to pass? It is too early to answer this question. However, one thing is certain: if unions do not take advantage of this space, other forms of representation and collective action will. These alternatives include increased legislation and blatantly manipulative efforts to reconstruct corporate cultures. One critical factor in shaping the future will be how unions themselves *choose* to relate to these new forms of work organization. That is, whether unions judge them as central or marginal to union survival and growth; as inherently good, evil, neutral, or contingent upon circumstances; and as immutable or subject to influence.

This book examines the relationship between unions and new forms of work organization through the lens of a single, but very significant case – local 800 of the Energy and Chemical Workers Union. ECWU local 800 represents workers at the Shell chemical plant in Sarnia, Canada. This plant, designed according to the principles of socio-technical systems (sts) thinking, is arguably the most advanced example to date of a new form of work organization in North America. More important, local 800 has made the initial and ongoing design of the chemical plant's work organization its central task. As a consequence, local 800 has shaped the work organization in a direction consistent with a democratic vision of the workplace. Significantly, this has entailed local 800 making fundamental changes in some of industrial unionism's long-established traditions, policies, and practices.

The experience of local 800 is not presented as a model from which general principles can be developed and widely applied.

However, the experience is not so unusual as to have no relevance beyond the boundaries of local 800. At the very least, the local 800 case illustrates that the socio-technical systems approach to new forms of work organization and a strong independent union can be mutually reinforcing rather than mutually exclusive. This is significant as the evidence is mounting (e.g., Pasmore 1988) that the sts approach is rapidly growing in popularity. In the view of this author, socio-technical systems and Japanese manufacturing are the main contenders to succeed Taylorism.

Local 800's story is offered as a practical contribution to the development of a union philosophy and strategy concerning new forms of work organization. For economic, social, and technological reasons, the widespread diffusion of these new forms, at least in manufacturing, is merely a matter of time. Unions will confront them in organizing drives and in long-unionized workplaces, in good economic times and in bad, and when dealing with both 'pro' and 'anti' union managements. However, the exact nature of these forms, let alone what and whose interests they will ultimately serve, is much more uncertain. Accordingly, the development of an independent union position concerning new forms of work organization is one of the most pressing and promising challenges facing unions today. This position must include a union vision of, and language for, the post-Taylorist future and a union competence in making this vision concrete. Furthermore, this position must enable unions to relate to new forms of work organization in a manner which strengthens the bonds between workers and unions and between workplace and societal change. To develop this position, unions must first understand the shop-floor implications of these new forms, their challenges to conventional unionism, and the possibilities and limitations of an effective union response. Without this grass-roots understanding, the efforts to develop the necessary changes in higher-level union, employer, and state policies, programs, and legislation will be misdirected. Accordingly, the focus of this book is at the point of production, the shop/office floor.

From a theoretical perspective, the aims of this book are twofold. First and foremost, the intent is to enrich the socio-technical systems perspective on organization design by drawing upon some of the ideas central to negotiations theory. Bridging the gaps between these (and other) disciplines is critical if social science is to contribute in a significant way to the current transformation of the workplace. Similarly, organizations which survive and prosper in the future will be ones where the boundaries between the production engineering, human resources, industrial relations, and other functions are recast.

The second aim is to encourage Canadians and Americans working in the socio-technical tradition to (re)discover some of their discipline's conceptual roots and fundamental values. The sts approach to organization theory has its origins in the work of Eric Trist and his Tavistock colleagues in the coal-mines of Britain. As David Herbst (1985) has pointed out, it is worth noting it was the miners and their union who 'invented' the semi-autonomous work group. The researchers supplied the term. Furthermore, the first large-scale 'test' and development of socio-technical systems thinking was the Norwegian Industrial Democracy Project, a joint union/ management undertaking. This project, as conceived by Einar Thorsrud and Fred Emery, took as its point of departure not the improvement of organization effectiveness but the development of participatory or direct democracy. Its overall aim was to begin a process of democratizing the western industrialized world.

After its voyage to North America, however, democracy disembarked as quality of working life. For many, the term QWL is more acceptable than democracy and this has no doubt facilitated some positive, concrete developments, especially on the shop and office floor. However, the term conceals as much as it reveals and has contributed to obscuring the democratic dimension which lies at the heart of the socio-technical approach. Furthermore, more than a few consultants and behavioural scientists have been willing to apply some of the sts ideas on designing effective work systems in the service of developing 'union-free environments.' Such a misuse of social-science knowledge is incompatible with the values of a democratic society.

This book is divided into six chapters. Chapter 1 argues that industrial unionism cannot be separated from the traditional approach to work organization – scientific management. Consequently, as this traditional approach is replaced, some of industrial unionism's basic tenets are no longer valid. Chapter 2 describes the initial and flawed approaches developed by industrial unions in an effort to deal with post-Taylorist forms of work organization. Chapter 3, 4, and 5 describe and analyse in detail the approach developed by ECWU local 800 in responding to the innovative work organization of the Shell chemical plant. This description and analysis strongly suggest that there is a feasible alternative to the 'non-union future' mentioned above. The final chapter briefly discusses, in both theoretical and practical terms, the relevance of the local 800 case beyond the chemical plant.

NEW FORMS OF
WORK ORGANIZATION

1 Industrial Unionism and the Legacy of Scientific Management

The Historical Context

A major achievement of the industrial age was the perfection of an organizational form, the technocratic bureaucracy (Trist 1981) which was suited to a world of mass production, standardized products, mechanization, and a poorly educated labour force. This form, which combined and made concrete the ideas of Weber (1947) and Taylor (1911), soon became so prevalent it took on the properties of an organizational paradigm (Kuhn 1962).[1] As a paradigm, the technocratic bureaucracy represents a set of beliefs, values, concepts, and techniques for organization design. It has become so strong a filter for both the appreciation (Vickers 1965) and consideration of design alternatives that many people have been unable to concieve of any other frame of reference.

This traditional paradigm follows the technological imperative. People are regarded simply as an extension of technology, as expendable spare parts. Simple tasks requiring narrow skills are equated to jobs. Control is achieved through layers of supervision, staff specialists, and formal procedures. An autocratic management style is dominant; competition is the key cultural value. Alienation and low risk-taking are common.

Unions were initially extremely hostile to this paradigm of organization. Spectacular strikes often accompanied the introduction of Taylorism[2] into plants (Aitken 1960). Unions in the United States successfully lobbied for the creation of congressional hearings to investigate its application. The report for the United States

Commission on Industrial Relations, among other criticisms, described Taylor's ideas and practices as anti-union (Hoxie 1915).

However, within a few years, unions not only accommodated themselves to this paradigm; in some cases they became its advocates (Jacoby 1983). The American Federation of Labour, for example, at its 1925 convention enthusiastically embraced Taylorism (Heckscher 1981). Union policies and practices (e.g., detailed contracts, work rules, and enforcement procedures) reflect and incorporate significant aspects of the paradigm (Slichter 1941; Chamberlain 1948; Nadworny 1955). In Canada, as late as 1984, the International Ladies Garment Workers Union ILGWU), concerned about the job security of its members, trained management personnel in union-sponsored courses in effective time and motion study.[3] According to Merkle (1980) scientific management was an 'integral part of the compromise engineered between business and labour' (247). Until quite recently, studies of unions (e.g., Gerschenfeld and Schmidt 1982) take as given the pervasive and integral presence and impact of this paradigm of organization.

However, dramatic change – intense, often world-wide competition often on the basis of quality, lead times, and product/service customization as well as costs (Abernathy, Clark, and Kantrow 1981), shifts in product markets (Piore and Sabel 1984), new technologies (Hirschhorn 1984), rapid technology transfer (Cohen and Zysman 1987), and changes in people's values and expectations (e.g., Davis 1980; Kanter 1978; Laberge 1978) – seriously threatens the viability of this paradigm. The environment is now turbulent (Emery and Trist 1964). The higher levels of interdependence, complexity, and uncertainty found in this environment surpass the limits within which the technocratic bureaucracy was designed to function.

Over the past twenty years, more adaptive forms of organization have been developed (e.g., Walton 1984; Mansell 1987a). Together, they suggest a new organizational pattern designed according to the concepts and principles of open, socio-technical systems thinking (Trist and Bamforth 1951; Emery 1959b). Descriptions of many of these new forms of organization often either ignore (e.g., Abernathy, Clark, and Kantrow 1983) or barely acknowledge (e.g., Kochan, Katz, and McKersie 1986) the concepts and principles of socio-technical systems thinking. It is the contention of this writer, however, that at the levels of the shop/office floor and enterprise, many of the central features of these new forms reflect socio-technical systems concepts and principles. Japanese production methods which are rapidly gaining in popularity in North American manufacturing are a case in point. Cole (1979) in his analysis of the Japanese labour market observes:

The Japanese efforts do have many parallels to the new approaches being explored in Western Europe. In particular, the methods developed at the Tavistock Institute in London and applied in Norway and Sweden through the work of Einar Thorsrud appear quite similar (Emery and Trist 1969). The emphasis in their approaches is on the development of the organization as an 'open socio-technical system' which focuses on the interaction of social and technical factors. The aim is to develop small work groups which maintain a high level of independence and autonomy. As a consequence it is expected that jobs will be enriched, individual responsibility increased, and learning possibilities enhanced. These same statements could be applied to the Japanese efforts. (20)

There are, however, crucial differences in terms of both values and concepts between the Japanese and sts approaches to work design. For example, socio-technical systems thinking puts far more emphasis on adapting technology to people. Accordingly, in the auto industry, Japanese team-based plants still have a traditional fixed-pace assembly line while in several sts team plants, such as Volvo in Sweden, the proposed Saturn complex in the United States, and General Motors plants in Oshawa, Canada, the traditional assembly line has been replaced by automated guided vehicles which free up workers from being tied to the technology. Furthermore, work redesign in Japan would appear to emphasize enriching the horizontal rather than the vertical dimension of jobs. The sts approach to job design typically encompasses both dimensions.

Trist (1981) argues that these innovative forms of organization indicate the emergence of a new paradigm of organization which, over time, may displace the old. In the emerging paradigm, people are regarded as complementary to technology. They are valued for their unique capacities for appreciative and evaluative judgment and seen as a resource to be developed. Jobs are replaced by roles demanding flexibility and multiple skills. Control is achieved through internal regulation and the redistribution of power among individuals and groups. A participative management style is dominant, collaboration a key cultural value. Commitment and innovation are the norm. Trist paints a positive picture. There is more than a little evidence to support his vision (e.g., Pasmore 1988). But as indicated in the preface, a different sort of post-Taylorist world may well emerge. It is this writer's belief that the support and active involvement of organized labour are necessary if Trist's vision is to become widespread.

The new paradigm is not yet mature. The most detailed accounts are at the level of the job and the work group (Emery 1977, 1978). However, there has been sufficient theoretical and practical progress that at the level of the establishment many of the new paradigm's underlying design principles have been identified. The following comparison of these principles with those underlying the old paradigm indicates the fundamental and irreconcilable differences between the two paradigms. This comparison, which draws heavily on Cherns (1976) and Davis (1977), is summarized in table 1.

Design Principles of the New and Old Paradigms of Organization

Before pursuing this comparison it is necessary to sort out some of the theoretical confusion surrounding socio-technical systems thinking and to sketch some of its underlying concepts. The sts approach is often equated to group theory, in particular that of semi-autonomous work groups. However, as Gustavsen (1986) points out, this is incorrect. As developed by Fred Emery and Eric Trist the socio-technical approach draws upon an eclectic set of theories. These include, in addition to the more well known ideas about the organization of production systems (Trist and Bamforth 1951), systems theory as applied to the enterprise as a whole (Emery 1959a), social ecology (Emery and Trist 1964, 1973), and Selznick's (1957) concept of institutional leadership. As Gustavsen points out, Emery's aim was to create 'a total theory: a theory encompassing all important aspects of development on the level of society, and for that matter the whole Western, industrialized world' (462). Central to this theory was the view that work organization held the key to democratizing not only the workplace but society at large. A review of this total theoretical framework is beyond the scope of this book. The interested reader is referred to Gustavsen (1986). The following comparison of design principles of the old and new paradigms deals with enterprise as a place of work, a central but not the only component of the sts approach.

There is no one best way to conceptualize organizations. As Morgan (1986) so vividly portrays, organizations can be thought of as everything from complex machines, to instruments of exploitation, to networks of information. In the socio-technical perspective, organizations are viewed first and foremost as places of work – where inputs are transformed into outputs. Such a perspective does not assume that organizations are as functionally unified as, say, the human body. Nor does it deny the existence of conflict within organizations and society at large. It does, however, focus attention on a fundamental and undeniable fact of organizational life – organizations are systems since the transformation of inputs to outputs necessarily involves interdependencies among the parts of an organization. The sts perspective is particularly illuminating at a time when the process by which inputs are transformed is itself being dramatically transformed.

Organizations which can be described as socio-technical are directly dependent on their material means and resources for their outputs. 'Their core interface consists of the relations between a nonhuman system and a human system' (Trist 1981, 12). It is the recognition of the significance of this interface and the manner in which it is designed (discussed below) which is the foundation of the socio-technical concept. Not all social systems are socio-technical. Emery (1959) distinguishes between operative and regulative institutions reserving the term socio-technical for the former.

As a system, an operative organization is made up of a set of interrelated parts that transform inputs (e.g., raw materials, knowledge) into outputs (e.g., goods and services). In socio-technical systems terms, the two most important parts of the organization are the technical subsystem and the social subsystem. The former consists of the equipment, tools, and techniques used to convert inputs into outputs. The definition of technical subsystem is not limited to machines. Consequently the socio-technical concept applies to both goods and service producing organizations.[4] The social subsystem includes the vertical and horizontal division of work, its co-ordination, conflict resolution processes, and mechanisms for maintaining the organization over time (e.g., recruiting, training). This definition of the social system illustrates that the sts approach views organizations as mini-societies as well as transforming agencies. According to the socio-technical approach, 'the technical and social subsystems are independent of each other in the sense that the former follows the laws of the natural sciences while the latter follows the "laws" of the human sciences and is a purposeful system' (Trist 1981, 24). This latter point underscores the fact that, contrary to some interpretations, the systems perspective of Emery and Trist went well beyond the limitations of using an organismic analogy to understand organizations. As Girth Higgin has pointed out, this criticism is more properly directed to Rice's (1958) version of sts.

An organization's technical and social subsystems are related in that both are required for the transformation of an input into an output. Their relationship represents 'a coupling of dissimilars ... in which the distinctive characteristics of each must be respected else their contradictions will intrude and their complementarities will remain unrealized' (Trist 1981, 24). As the comparison of design principles which follows indicates, there is considerable choice as to how to couple an organization's social and technical subsystems. However, not all choices are 'equal.' From an sts perspective economic performance and social indicators (e.g., human dignity) are, to a large degree, dependent on the goodness of fit between the social and technical subsystems. Kochan (1988) reports empirical evidence supporting this hypothesis. From a production management perspective, Abernathy, Clark, and Kantrow (1983) make a similar argument: 'Integrating people into the manufacturing process so that their skills and abilities become and *remain* a point of competitive leverage ... remains the central unmet challenge of American manufacturing' (83, emphasis in original).

The socio-technical approach views organizations as open systems, acknowledging that they do not exist in a vacuum but are embedded in the larger society. As open systems, organizations are subject to external forces (e.g., competition, cultural values) often beyond their control. The performance of any organization is, therefore, partially dependent upon its ability to sense, influence, and adjust to the dynamic aspects of its environment.

With these basic concepts as background I will turn to the comparison of the key design principles underlying socio-technical systems thinking and those upon which traditional forms of organization are based. These design principles, for the most part, focus on the content rather than the process of organization design. Recently, Bjorn Gustavsen and his colleagues at the Work Research Institutes in Oslo and the Swedish Center for Working Life in Stockholm have shifted the focus in the sts thinking away from structural or content theory 'and towards *generative* theory: theory about how to create patterns of organization' (Gustavsen 1986, 467). Gustavsen's work has been influenced by Habermas's (1972) theory of communicative competence, the 'later' Wittgenstein's (1961) philosophy of language, and the French poststructuralists (e.g. Foucault 1972). Such a heady mix promises to overcome the theoretical stagnation Barko and Pasmore (1986) observe in their recent review of the state of development of socio-technical systems theory.

The shift in focus noted above from content to process may eventually mean that the design principles of the paradigm take on a less prominent position in sts thinking. However, it is difficult to imagine them becoming unimportant. There is a strong relationship between content and process in any system. Obviously, for example, the capacity to create patterns of organizations is, in part, dependent upon a basic structure which is flexible.

The socio-technical approach to organization design rests on nine key principles: redundancy of functions, joint optimization, participatory self-design, minimal critical specification, variance control, boundary location, design and human values, support system congruence, and incompletion.

In order to cope with variety, all organizations must possess redundancy or excess capacity. The alternative is an organization with a fixed repertoire of responses appropriate to a limited set of

TABLE 1
NEW AND OLD PARADIGM DESIGN PRINCIPLES

NEW PARADIGM	OLD PARADIGM
Redundancy of functions	Redundancy of parts
Joint optimization	Technical imperative
Participative design	Exclusive design
Minimal critical specification	Total specification
Local control of variances	Remote control of variances
Boundary location	Boundary location
A socio-technical whole	Technology, territory, time
Design and human values	Design and human values
Intrinsic and extrinsic properties of jobs	Extrinsic properties of jobs
Support system congruence	Support system incongruence
Incompletion	Completion

environmental conditions. According to Pierce (quoted in Emery 1977) with each arithmetic increase in redundancy the reliability of an organization tends to increase exponentially. *The principle of redundancy of functions* (Emery 1977) states that excess capacity be achieved by building redundant functions into the parts of an organization, for example, the multi-skilling of workers and/or work groups. The same function can be performed in different ways by using a different combination of parts. There are, therefore, several routes to the same goal. Furthermore, since each part is itself a purposeful system (Ackoff and Emery 1972) each can set and reset its own functions as the situation demands. Overall, an organization's capacity to cope flexibly and quickly with a variety of issues is considerable. The principle of redundancy of function is, perhaps, the most significant of the sts design principles. Pava (1981) labels it as one of two 'bed-rock alternatives.' The other, the principle of redundancy of parts, underlies the old paradigm of organization.

Under the principle of redundancy of parts excess capacity is achieved by adding redundant parts to the system. Control mechanisms (specialized parts) determine which parts are active or inactive for a particular response. If the control is to be reliable it must also have redundant parts and the question of a further control emerges. Under this design principle, reliability is secured at the cost of providing or maintaining the redundant parts; hence the tendency is toward continual reduction of the functions of each part. Therefore, in most organizations responsibilities are broken down so that the basic elements are as simple and hence inexpensive as possible (e.g., unskilled workers assigned to narrow jobs with correspondingly low replacement costs and short training times). These parts are then reintegrated through a special control mechanism, vertical supervision, which itself is also fragmented, leading to still further layers of control. This results in the familiar organizational pyramid with workers at the bottom supporting an ascending hierarchy of control. Overall, an organization's capacity to cope flexibly and quickly with a variety of issues is not great.

The principle of joint optimization (Emery 1959) states that organization's technical and social subsystems must be designed (and continuously redesigned) to establish the best fit between the two.[5] Attempts to optimize the performance of one without regard to the other will result in the suboptimization of the whole. While the effective functioning of both subsystems is vital to organizational performance, their overall fit is what is critical. In a similar vein, Reich (1987) notes:

One of the key lessons to come out of the General Motors–Toyota joint venture in California is that the Japanese automaker does not rely on automation and technology to replace workers in the plant. In fact, human workers still occupy the most critical jobs – those where judgement and evaluation are essential. Instead, Toyota uses technology to allow workers to focus on those important tasks where choices have to be made. Under this approach, technology gives workers the chance to use their imagination and their insight on behalf of the company. (82)

In contrast, the old paradigm follows the technical imperative. The social subsystems are subordinate to the technical system. The results are often serious – for example, the famous Lordstown strike – and could well be catastrophic as demonstrated at the Three Mile Island Nuclear Power Plant. The General Motors Lordstown, Ohio, assembly plant, considered in the early 1970s to be the ultimate in technical sophistication, was plagued by wildcat strikes, sabotage, and abnormal high absenteeism. Management and union responded (unsuccessfully) to the situation by negotiating higher wage rates. The underlying problem, the failure to synchronize the technical and social systems, was never acknowledged, let alone addressed (Davis 1983). In the Three Mile Island case, testimony presented to the commission of inquiry indicated that the plant was built with the belief that reliability and safety could be achieved only by designing the technical system so as to create a 'fool-proof' system. The social system consisted 'of a steep hierarchy, fractioned work, and truncated responsibilities sanctioned by union management relationships and agreements' (Davis 1983, 10). Operators were restricted to manual work (e.g., moving levers) and engineers, who monopolized all mental work, were not permitted to adjust meters or turn knobs, jobs classified as manual work. Furthermore, no operator or engineer knew how to operate more than a small segment of the plant. It is no wonder that a near disaster developed when a crisis occurred (Hirschhorn 1982; Davis 1983).

The principle of participative design states that an organization should be designed by all its members, and not simply by an élite few. This is logistically feasible in existing organizations. In new organizations, while significant decisions must be made before most employees are hired, many decisions can and should be left until staffing is completed. In both cases specialists should participate, not dominate. Under the old paradigm participation in organizational design is usually the exclusive domain of a few senior managers assisted by internal and/or external specialists.

The principle of minimal critical specification (Herbst 1962) states that no more should be specified than is absolutely essential. This applies to all aspects of an organization (e.g., tasks, roles, objectives) and is essential for enhancing an organization's capacity for adapting to change. Most organizations are designed according to the old paradigm's principle of complete specification. The resulting rules, if strictly applied (as in a union work-to-rule campaign), totally inhibit effective day-to-day operations as well as block strategic adaption.

The principle of local control of variances states that the information, skills, and authority needed to control things that could go wrong (i.e., variances) in the technical subsystem should be located where the variance is likely to occur. Statistical process control (spc) is an example of a technique which embodies this principle. However, to be fully consistent with this and other sts design principles, the tasks of data collection, data analysis, and process adjustment would have to be integrated into the same role. In traditionally designed organizations the capacity for managing variances is usually remote from the locations in which they occur. Vertical lines of command are emphasized; slow responses, indifferent workers, and low performance are often the result. According to *Business Week* (8 June 1987) the typical u.s. factory spends 25 per cent of its budget on finding and correcting mistakes.

The principle of boundary location states that the boundaries of organizational units (e.g., production, maintenance) should be located so that each unit controls inputs, produces identifiable outcomes, and possesses the requisite response capabilities in terms of skills information, and competencies (in part, a function of the principle of local control of variances). The more the co-ordination and control of activities within the unit are the responsibility of its members, the more the role of the supervisor/manager is freed up to concentrate on boundary activities (e.g., co-ordination with other units). In favourable circumstances the unit's members can manage their own boundaries. The supervisor/manager then becomes a resource to the unit. According to the old paradigm, an organization's boundaries are usually drawn on the basis of one or more of three criteria: technology, territory, and time (Miller 1959). An unintended consequence is often boundaries which interfere with the sharing of knowledge and experience necessary for effective performance.

The principle of design and human values states that autonomy and discretion, opportunity to learn and continue learning on the job, optimal variety, social support and recognition, sense of meaningful contribution, and prospects for a meaningful future are basic requirements people have of their work (Emery and Thorsrud 1976). Furthermore, the principle states that jobs and organizations should be designed to fulfil these requirements. Under the old paradigm, people's requirements of work are assumed to be limited to those associated with the extrinsic properties of jobs (e.g., pay). The sts school has been criticized for basing, in part, its argument for organization redesign on the existence of general human psychological needs (e.g., Silverman 1971; Gustavsen 1980). As the latter points out, the empirical evidence for such a claim is scanty at best. And Berner (1986) argues that the concept of generalized human needs ignores the social and collective character of working life.

On the one hand these criticisms are overstated and not altogether accurate. While there may be no general theory of human needs, the need for people to exercise some control over their day-to-day life rests on a somewhat more firm empirical footing (Gustavsen 1987). In addition, the practical use of the sts view of human needs has been more as a tool for stimulating discussion and debate rather than as a rigid blueprint for redesign. In this writer's experience, this tool has proved very useful in the field as it has high face validity with managers and workers. Finally, many North American applications of sts concepts (especially in new plants) have not ignored, but in fact have acknowledged and capitalized on, the social and collective character of working life. Indeed, a central problem facing unions in organizing these new plants is labour's inability to articulate a collective vision of the workplace which is not only superior to that of management but as well is consistent with today's economic, social, and technological developments.

On the other hand, the above criticisms are to the point. The focus on social-psychological factors has contributed to sts theory and practice, at least in North America, downplaying the importance of cultural and political aspects of the workplace. As Berner (1986) points out: 'The satisfaction of individual needs is neither the only nor the best criterion for designing better working conditions' (96). Von Otter (quoted in Berner 1986), for example, argues that changes in work organization should be grounded in the rights of workers to formulate their own goals in accordance with their own collective views and norms. This writer shares these criticisms and is doubtful that further conceptual and practical progress in the sts school can be made by a continued reliance on psychological theory. In this writer's view, the most significant developments in the sts field are currently to be found in Scandinavia, where both theory and practice are more informed by democratic than psychological theory (e.g., Gustavsen and Englestad 1986).

The principle of support system congruence states that an organization's support systems (e.g., accounting, payment, performance assessment, training) should be designed to reinforce the behaviour which the overall organizational structure is designed to elicit. Kochan, Katz and McKersie (1986) make a similar point from an industrial relations perspective. They argue that for new forms of organization to survive over time an enterprise's conflict management and work organization must not only support and reinforce each other, but also be congruent with overall management and labour interactions.

One of the more interesting developments in American manufacturing today is the attempt to revamp cost accounting and capital budgeting procedures so that they are consistent with today's economic and technological realities. Traditional procedures, for example, have focused primarily on savings from direct labour to justify capital investment. But today in many industries, labour represents only 10–15 per cent of production costs. Consequently, non-direct cost areas, many of which are difficult to quantify, must be considered. According to *Business Week* (27 April 1987) a task force including representatives from the Big Eight accounting firms and thirty industrial companies is trying to develop a framework for evaluating how factors such as higher quality and improved delivery times can improve market share and revenues.

In the old paradigm, however, congruence is not required as the organization is viewed as a collection of discrete parts rather than as an integrated system. What is assumed is that the behaviour of an organization is simply the sum or aggregate of its individual elements (Herbst 1985). As there is no need to take into account the relations among the elements, the optimization of each rather than the whole becomes an end in itself. In many cases, therefore, some support systems run counter to the organization's overall objectives and values. For example, organizations committed to developing their managers sometimes employ appraisal systems that are more punitive than developmental even when effective management development is central to organization growth and survival.

Finally, *the principle of incompletion* states that design is a never-ending process. As soon as a design is implemented some of its unforeseeable consequences and the changing environment will make redesign a necessity. Design and operations are seen as a continuous process. Ongoing redesign is not an indication of failure. Rather, it is a response to the fact that things (including people's expectations and objectives) change. This notion is in sharp contrast to traditional thinking, where design is a project with a discrete beginning and end. The need for occasional redesign is seen as the result of a failure in design or operations, two related but independent functions. The significance of the principle of incompletion will increase as tomorrow's organizations become 'more and more to resemble a conglomerate of continuously changing organizational patterns. [Accordingly] specific patterns will be transient and temporary in nature.' (Gustavsen 1986, 373).[6]

Such a dramatic discontinuity as described above suggests serious consequences for unions. For example, Kochan and Katz (1983) argue that the extensive diffusion of new forms of work organization would fundamentally alter the character of the U.S. collective bargaining and industrial relations systems at the plant level. In turn, these new forms would 'pose severe challenges for the local union.' In a more recent work (Kochan, Katz, and McKersie 1986) the authors conclude that 'wherever plants were designed and run on the new human resource management models they were essentially immune to unionization in the 1970s' (64). Many of these plants had an explicit goal to remain union-free (e.g., Poza 1980). Accordingly, some opponents of worker participation programs have seized upon the link between new forms of work organization and union avoidance strategies as de facto proof of the 'real' motives of management. However, as Kochan and Piore (1984) note, inasmuch as these forms are a consequence of market and technological changes, they 'have a logic that goes considerably deeper than a simple union avoidance strategy' (183).

Some Limits of Industrial Unionism

The response by the labour movement to the Shell chemical plant's organization design and collective-bargaining system – a response on occasion emotional, irrational, and hostile – underlines just how severe a challenge new forms of work organization offer to present-day unions. For example:

- The labour college of the Canadian Labour Congress literally threw out the ECWU national representative who services local 800 when he attempted to defend his union's behaviour in the chemical plant.
- The president of another ECWU local who claimed to have read the Shell local 800 collective agreement in detail emphatically insisted (contrary to fact) that there was no seniority clause concerning lay-offs.
- Members of the Sarnia district labour council continually ridiculed the two delegates from local 800, saying they represented the 'Shell comical plant.'
- The shop chairman of a large CAW local stormed out of the room, unable to finish listening to a presentation by the vice-president of local 800, once it was established there was no seniority clause covering 'promotion' in the chemical plant. The chairman accused the presenter of being a traitor to the union movement.

These responses must be seen in the light of the use of new forms of work organization by many companies, particularly in the United States, to weaken unions (e.g., Parker 1985). However, the nature of the reactions to the chemical plant's innovations can also be explained by the fact that they challenge some of industrial unionism's core tenets. These tenets, separately and as a system, incorporate, reflect, and support Taylorism. Local 800 was forced to abandon them when confronted with the challenge of representing workers in a post-Taylorist workplace. The experience of local 800 suggests there is an irreconcilable mismatch between the socio-technical systems approach to work organization and these tenets of industrial unionism:[7]

- job control is the best way to achieve job and income security
- indirect representation is the only realistic form of representation
- strict uniformity is a necessary condition for maintaining solidarity
- all conflict is distributive conflict

– regulation of the union-management relationship is best handled by rules

These tenets will be discussed separately and as a system in relation to both scientific management and the new paradigm of organization. Finally, craft unionism and its approach to collective bargaining which flourished prior to the advent of scientific management will be briefly described. I will return to the idea of different forms of unionism again in chapters 4 and 6 in the discussion of the meaning of the ECWU local 800 experience, and its implications for unions in general.

Job Control

At both national and shop-floor levels, the labour relations systems in Canada and the United States rely on contractually defined procedures to regulate the relationship between labour and management. These procedures are heavily focused on job control (Katz 1984). For one thing, wages are explicitly tied to jobs and not to worker characteristics. In addition, contracts spell out in great detail elaborate job classification systems including the exact requirements of each detailed job and the seniority rights that are tied to a job ladder which guides promotions, transfers, and lay-offs (Piore 1982). Unions, therefore, control job and income security by negotiating and administering a set of rules that determine how lay-offs are handled and the remaining work is allocated and how workers move from one job to another. According to Kochan and Piore (1984), under the system of job control 'Industrial democracy is reduced to a particular form of industrial jurisprudence in which work and disciplinary standards are clearly defined and fairly administered and disputes over the application of rules and customs are impartially adjudicated' (179).

The development of job control as a central union strategy for securing job and income security has its origin in labour's response to the emergence of the internal labour market (Doeringer and Piore 1971). The term 'internal labour market' draws attention to the fact that in many organizations the 'pricing and allocation functions of the market take place within rather than outside of the establishment' (Osterman 1984, 2). A detailed review of the factors underlying the development of internal labour markets is beyond the scope of this book. Jacoby (1984) points out the important role played by unions, governments, and 'progressive' personnel officials in supplanting the 'drive' system of the external labour market in the early days of U.S. industry with today's widely accepted and lauded internal labour market.

It is important to bear in mind that the internal labour market developed in the context of scientific management and in the period between the decline of craft unions at the turn of the century and the emergence of industrial unionism in the 1930s and 1940s. As Kochan and Piore (1984) point out, industrial unionism and its strategy of job control 'can best be understood as an adaptation to the technology and managerial practices that American industry had developed for the mass production of standardized goods. Work had previously been broken down into a discrete set of clearly defined jobs by industrial engineers following the scientific management practices'[8] ... Thus (industrial) unions found many of the mechanisms already in place and sought to ensure conformity with established principles in order to curtail favouritism and capriciousness in management' (180).

The internal labour market assisted industrial unions in regulating the competition from external labour markets. In turn, collective bargaining developed as the system for regulating the internal market. Since, as argued above, this internal market developed in the context of Taylorism, unions, unable to challenge this framework, focused their efforts on the regulation of narrow, fixed jobs. They approached this task from the strong tradition of job conciousness unionism based on the notion of workers 'property rights' to jobs (Perlman 1928) which had its origin in craft union practices. This tradition refers to the strategy of fighting for tight job classifications to gain job and income security. If one accepts – or is forced to accept – the logic of scientific management, this strategy makes sense. It provides workers' security in a system where they are valued only for what they do, not for what they have done in the past or might do in the future.

Tight classifications offer workers some hope of vested rights, some respite from being treated as interchangeable parts. Strict job hierarchies allow unions to insist on equal pay for equal work and promotion on the basis of seniority (Kochan and Katz 1983). If seniority provisions can be extended across departments, plants, and companies, they can offer some 'return on investment' for the years a worker spends with a company. Furthermore, if job descriptions are kept tight, workers cannot be forced to double-up and do another worker out of a job (Roberts 1984). However, the job control strategy welded industrial unions and scientific management to one another. It legitimated and generated consent to a labour process emptied of skill (Buroway 1979). A case in point is the American steel industry.

In steel, the triumph of industrial unionism did not change a job structure so denuded of skill that the job of a melter, the most highly skilled job in the open-hearth departments at the turn of the century, required only six to eight weeks' training for a raw recruit to master (Jeans 1902, cited in Stone 1975). According to Stone (1975), the impact of industrial unionism on the industry job structure was threefold. First, in co-operation with management, it further streamlined the hierarchical, fractioned job system into a rigid ladder of 30 job classifications in which the skill difference between classes was more apparent than real. Second, the union demanded and won a say in the development and operation of training programs related to these narrow job classes though it did not question the content of the training. Third, it did away with favouritism by insisting that seniority be used to regulate promotion and bumping. These three developments served to strengthen the job structure, giving it the union's blessing and according it on a basis of fairness rather than at the foremen's whim. This pattern was repeated in many other industries in the United States. For example, Chinoy (1965) in his classic *Automobile Workers and the American Dream* describes a job ladder system, which, despite covering more than 500 separate job classifications, 'left workers with little chance to exercise judgement, assume responsibility or develop significant skills.' (34).

Stone argues that the creation of job ladders pitted each worker against all the others in rivalry for achievement and undercut any feelings of unity which might develop among them. Jacoby (1984) counters this argument, pointing out that internal job ladders probably reduced rivalry among workers as they undercut the arbitrary power of an often tyrannical foreman. Regardless of the interpretation, industrial unions – while curtailing management's power to treat people as interchangeable parts – embraced a job structure which embodies this basic tenet of scientific management.

Job control was a rational and successful strategy for industrial unions in the context of Taylorism. That is to say, it was not without its weaknesses. By insisting on precise definitions of narrow repetitive jobs, for example, unions offered management a map which facilitated mechanization (Warrian 1980). Job control can be seen as one example of less powerful groups in an organization protecting themselves through bureaucratic regulations. As Crozier (1964) points out, the removal of such regulations can have negative effects on groups who lack other means to exercise power. Interestingly, Scandinavian unions who, unlike their North American counterparts, exercise considerable political power did not develop a strategy of job control in the face of Taylorism. This is a major reason why U.S. and Canadian unions have been reluctant to abandon the job control strategy. However, within the framework of the new paradigm, the strategy of job control makes much less sense. According to a study commissioned by the United States National Research Council (1986), advanced manufacturing technology tends to integrate previously discrete work activities, generally enhances skill requirements, and demands a quicker response time in the event of malfunction. Accordingly, management is reducing the number and broadening the scope of job classes, organizing work in teams, and delegating considerable authority to shop-floor operators. Pay is often linked to the accumulation of skills and knowledge which are usually superfluous to the job at hand. In sum, workers are valued as a resource to be developed. These developments signal not just the end but a reversal of Taylorism. Consequently, they directly challenge a strategy of job control. Indeed, in a post-Taylorist workplace, the concept of a job will be as misleading as the unfortunate use of the word 'jobs' in scientific management to describe what are, in fact, tasks. Such a fundamental shift in basic concepts will require just as fundamental a response from unions.

Indirect Representation

Union constitutions empower the membership as a whole with ultimate authority. However, Gulowsen (1982) argues that unions inevitably fall victim to Michels's (1962) 'iron law of oligopoly.' 'It is organization which gives birth to the dominion of the elected over the electors, of the mandataries over the mandators, of the delegates over the delegators. Who says organization says oligarchy' (365). In such circumstances the union membership participates periodically through the election of officers and ratification of contracts in much the same way that ordinary citizens participate in the political life of Canada and the United States. Except on official designated occasions, the few speak and act on behalf of the majority. According to Heckscher (1986), 'free discussions of internal conflicts, open expressions of disagreement are rare.' Heckscher goes on to argue that the reason that union leaders are reluctant to involve the membership in internal union affairs to any significant degree lies in the adversarial relationship between labour and management: 'they can't afford to be much more democratic than their opponents.' However, Taylorism is also a significant factor in explaining unions' preference for indirect or representative democracy. As Pateman (1970) and Mason (1982) argue, the 'effective' functioning of representative democracy – including unions and collective bargaining – requires an apathetic majority. This apathy is, in part, a consequence of a de-skilled and a segmented workforce. No wonder that many work redesign projects include extensive training of workers in the basics of problem-solving and communication. What more telling indication is there of the extent to which scientific management has undermined the most basic of human skills, thereby encouraging dependence on experts and elected officials?

This understandable bias in industrial unions toward representative participation is further exacerbated by the development of connective bargaining (Ulman 1974) which reflects and builds upon the old paradigm of organization. Connective bargaining involves the negotiation of wages, fringes, and some work conditions between a company and a national union, the latter connecting the company-side wage settlements in an industry via pattern bargaining. Working conditions and, to a lesser degree, some pay questions are also negotiated at the plant level with local unions. Until the recent severe economic downturn, connective bargaining was standard practice for major industries such as automobile, steel, and rubber. According to Katz (1984), in theory connective bargaining should result in considerable deviation in the area of working conditions, but in practice this has not been the case. Local unions, until very recently, have been unable to trade local work rules for pay changes and the national union in certain cases can veto many features of local agreements as well as strikes. Connective bargaining, therefore, shifts the level in the union at which issues are addressed to national rather than local representatives. Thus the rank and file are progressively distanced from the decision-making process.[9]

The centralization of power and separation of planning and execution characteristic of connective bargaining are the mirror image of their counterparts in scientific management. In fact, for both union and management, connective bargaining is a logical outcome of a system of organization which, at the level of a plant, is designed to inhibit innovation, flexibility, and discretion. For example, Kochan, Katz, and McKersie (1986) argue that the increase in the number of written grievances and issues raised in local negotiations at GM during the 1960s reflects in part 'the inability of the master national contract and central dealings between labour and management to attend to the myriad of problems that arose across the more than one hundred GM plants (39).

The new paradigm of organization is incompatible with the assumption that indirect representation is the only 'really' workable form of representation. Competitive pressures, especially for quality goods and services, 'demand' more complex behaviour on the part of workers (Gustavsen 1987). For example, workers and work groups resolve issues on their own (and are rewarded for doing so). Pushing issues 'up the line' is discouraged. These issues include not only day-to-day problems but the shaping of the values, norms, and rules which regulate the workplace – items typically handled virtually exclusively on the union side by elected officials. As Gustavsen points out, traditional methods of eliciting behaviour from workers – coercion and manipulation – are of limited use in dealing with such complex behaviour. Indeed, Abernathy, Clark, and Kantrow (1983) label these methods as 'poison' and possibly 'lethal to these who rely on (them)' (90). Instead agreements must be reached between labour and management. However, these agreements cannot be equated to traditional collective agreements which are negotiated by worker representatives. These new agreements 'demand more in terms of active participation from all concerned since they have the purpose of regulating behaviour rather than the frame conditions of behaviour' (Gustavsen 1987, 3). As a consequence, industrial unions are challenged to rethink the relation between direct and indirect representation. The extent of the challenge is captured by Heckscher (1986), who in his brief review of the union response to employee participation finds the 'local autonomy and decentralized decision making are profoundly disturbing to them (unions).'

Solidarity through Strict Uniformity

Historically, unions' preference for uniform treatment of their members as a means of attaining justice was understandable. They had had their fill of exceptions made on the basis of age, marital status, ethnicity, and region, not to mention bribes including the exchange of sexual favours. These had noting to do with the work at hand and, to a certain degree, were eliminated through union struggles (Roberts 1984). According to Slichter, Healy, and Livernash (as referred to in Kochan, Katz, and McKersie 1986) one of the major impacts of collective bargaining on management was 'the reduction in variability associated with the foreman-driven management system' (89).

Ironically, the unions' use of uniformity as a means of pursuing justice was co-opted into the service of scientific management. In turn, the proposition that the strict uniform treatment of members is a necessary condition for solidarity became a tenet of industrial unionism. However, this bias towards uniformity is at odds with the emphasis put on diversity in the sts approach to organization design. Consequently, a new basis for solidarity must be developed.

The achievement of justice through uniformity coincided with scientific management's drive for stability, predictability, and control. During the three decades following the Second World War, organizations prospered by producing standardized products for Mass markets (Reich 1983). Management concerned itself with organizing the routine 'normal' efforts of workers through the laying down of minimal standard requirements (Edwards 1979). (The requirements of 'high commitment' organizations characteristic of the new paradigm [Walton 1984] for exceptional effort, creativity, and initiative were not needed, elicited, or valued.) The pursuit of justice through uniformity was naturally co-opted by the systematic power of the 'invisible hand' of scientific management (Hyman 1981) into the pursuit of stability and control of plant life through uniformity. This co-option not only further assimilated the policy and practice of industrial unionism into the framework of scientific management, it led to the proposition that solidarity among workers is dependent upon their uniform treatment. The origin and development of seniority, one of the most revered 'principles' of unionism and the most common application of the notion of uniformity, is a good case in point.[10]

With varying degrees of comprehensiveness, seniority clauses are written into almost all private sector collective agreements. These clauses see to it that access to all job openings is regulated by years of service (i.e., seniority), which minimizes discrimination on the basis of ability, sex, ethnicity, or other strictly subjective considerations.

As a procedure that allows people to look forward to a larger share of 'goods' and a smaller share of 'bads' as a reward for years of service, seniority is as old and honoured as civilization itself (Gersuny 1982). It is especially well-adapted to the needs of an economy shaped by internal labour markets and stable product markets because it rewards lengthy service and reduces turnover. In the context of scientific management, seniority is the 'grease' that makes a job structure composed of detailed, narrow tasks largely denuded of challenge and discretion work smoothly. While it provides the worker with considerable security in and predictability about the future in such a work system it also helps ensure its survival by ensuring that workers have a vested interest in the system. Furthermore, it serves for industrial unions as important common ground on which to build the solidarity critical for pursuing their interest vis-à-vis management. To appreciate the dynamics of this process, it is useful to trace the origin and development of scientific management and seniority procedures in the light of two of the organization design principles discussed earlier in this chapter, redundancy of parts and redundancy of functions.

According to these principles, redundancy can be achieved either by treating people as replaceable parts or workhands or by endowing people with functions superfluous to the task at hand. In the era which preceded scientific management – at least for the skilled worker – the latter formed the basis for excess capacity. Thus, artisans owed their superior pay, working conditions, and power to their possession of 'superfluous' knowledge. Their long and rounded apprenticeship, their command over all the tricks of the trade, was their ticket to craftsman status. In order to handle the variations from one job to another, they needed to know more than they applied in any one job.

Taylor sought to reduce the power of the craftsmen and their unions by reducing their skill level to the task at hand.[11] He reasoned that by breaking down the combination of activities of a skilled job and reducing these activities to a series of separate tasks, management could gain control over the work process. Redundancy would be achieved through the use of people as replaceable parts. The very basis of the antagonism between scientific management and artisan-bred craft unions derived from this struggle for control of the workplace.

Craft unions tried to protect their members in this struggle by defining their jurisdiction in terms of 'universes of work' and by insisting on high standards of apprenticeship (Roberts 1984). The critical base upon which solidarity was built in this fight with management and its scientific management strategy was membership in a common trade. It was the whole which connected the parts (i.e. members) and, like a hologram, was in the parts although the parts could and did practise their trade in a variety of ways.

The protective walls which craft unions tried to build around their 'superfluous' knowledge were breached in all but the construction and printing trades, following a series of union set-backs from 1890 to 1930. With the destruction of craft unions in a heavy industry, the way was paved for organization according to the principle of replaceable parts. If a company faced a downturn, it had the flexibility to lay off relatively replaceable workers. If a company faced a rush of orders, it could hire extra workers. Workers who quit could be quickly replaced, with a minimum of training. Wages could be determined by the ease of replacement.

As discussed earlier, industrial unions won recognition in the 1930s and 1940s but were unable to overthrow a work system based on the principle of redundant parts. Instead, they bargained for elaborate seniority procedures to ensure fairness in the distribution of jobs within the system. However, these procedures not only bred an intense loyalty to and a vested interest in scientific management, they also formed the basis for the widespread acceptance of the position that uniformity was a necessary condition for developing worker solidarity. Workers accepted the dull, deadening jobs in their early years with the understanding that later on in their work life they would be entitled to the 'good' jobs. 'Good' meant not necessarily more challenge or autonomy, but work usually free of heavy labour, on days, or in a warm, dry setting. As a consequence, individual worker interests and the interests of scientific management were merged.

Seniority provided industrial unions with a key basis for solidarity in their ongoing struggle with management concerning the regulation of the work system. Uniformity (in this case seniority) and a common enemy are the only bases for solidarity in the disconnected world of scientific management. When there is no whole, let alone a whole which can be effectively and positively represented in its parts, then uniform treatment permits some degree of solidarity. In a similar vein, Heckscher (1981) notes that union representatives see themselves not as leaders of a solidarity and committed group with a sense of long term shared interests, but rather as trying to keep together a movement which can fragment very quickly' (237).

As most work design practitioners well know, any attempt to redesign seniority procedures (in part of or in whole) is considered a violation of a sacred trust. Emery (1978) labels these as workers' 'second lines of defence' whose original purpose and authors are long forgotten and whose unintended consequence is sometimes to blind workers to their own interest. Any individual or group which is deemed to be getting privileges which are not a 'right' by seniority is attacked by the rest of the membership – solidarity is threatened by differences. From this perspective, seniority rights are consistent with Herding's (1972) critique that the rise of employee rights is merely one aspect of the overall trend to impersonal treatment, equalization and elimination of individual discretion in modern society. When such a basic tenet of unions as solidarity is perceived to be threatened by differences, it is just a small step to the development of an attitude that any 'special treatment' which is not uniformly applied to all is by definition not in the interest of the whole. More than one work redesign project has failed because this dynamic has been ignored (e.g., Goodman and Dean 1981; Mansell and Rankin 1983). Dahrendorf's (quoted in Lawrence 1982) description of class solidarity based on uniformity makes a similar point while also implying a link to scientific management: 'It is within the little boxes which the division of labour has bequeathed us, a solidarity in other words which involves permanent concern with the boundary of one's own box, and thus with comparability. Such solidarity can be quite ruthless: it is a much stronger force for people than any appeal to over-riding common interests of an enterprise, a community, a nation.'

For some industrial unions, solidarity has become synonymous with and dependent upon uniformity. Exceptions, be they cafeteria plans for fringe benefits or affirmative action plans for minorities, cut across the grain of uniformity and are commonly rejected and resisted. New forms of work organization, however, challenge unions to rethink the proposition that solidarity is best achieved through uniformity. Smaller organizational units with greater autonomy, diversity within units traditionally managed by standard procedures, and more accommodation of individual differences in preference and capacity (Schlesinger and Walton 1977) – all of these run counter to the notion of uniform treatment and as a consequence undermine a traditional basis for worker solidarity.

The Nature of Conflict

The assumption on the part of unions that all conflict between labour and management is distributive in nature is based upon the widely shared view of labour as a commodity and the day-to-day actions that logically follow from this view. This particular view of labour and its understandably powerful influence on unions' thinking is aptly illustrated by the following quote from the history of a noted twentieth-century trade union, the United Mine and Mill Workers Union: ' "We buy many commodities", the corporate chief explained as he opened negotiations, "steel, mica, enamels. When we buy these things, we pay the lowest price we possibly can. We also need to buy your labour, it too is a commodity that we need. And we're going to buy it for the lowest price we can" ' (Walsh 1972, 2).

This win-lose approach to labour-management relations has in turn been assumed and structured by the legal foundations of the Canadian and American industrial relations system (Adams 1981; Lemelin 1981; Mansell 1980; White 1975). This legal tradition, in Canada a legacy of the divine rights of employers under Britain's Master Servant Act of 1634, in turn assigns to management all rights which are not specifically restricted by the collective agreement. This allocation of power in the workplace, known as the principle of residual rights, is the legal manifestation of the concept of labour as a commodity and established the priority of property over the principles of democracy (Beatty 1984). As Kochan, Katz, and McKersie (1986) point out, the high conflict/low trust pattern often associated with the handling of distributive or win/lose conflict can spill over into all the issues with which the two parties deal. This can lead to 'a cycle whereby conflicts involving some issues drive out the potential for cooperation and problem solving where the parties share common interest' (85).

Labour as a commodity to be exploited is, of course, a fundamental tenet of scientific management. The principle of residual rights, or managerial perogatives, as reflected in the standard management rights clause is virtually all collective agreements, not only formalizes this win-lose relationship between management and labour but is also a logical outcome of the separation of planning and doing inherent in Taylorism. The win-lose orientation to labour-management relations has been reinforced by the lengths (both legal and illegal) to which management has gone to prevent unionization of the workforce. It is not surprising, therefore, that unions have developed the position that in their relation with management, a gain for 'them' must be at the expense of 'us'.

However, a basic tenet of the new paradigm of organization is that labour is a resource to be developed. Organization design practitioners and managers talk of the 'mutuality of interests' between labour and management (Lawrence and Walton 1985). A few firms, emulating the Japanese, offer lifelong employment and do not lay off employees even when traditional economic circumstances would have dictated such a response (Jain and Ohtsu 1983). Such tendencies are no doubt related to the fact that the increase in capital costs relative to labour in all sectors of the economy limits the contribution to profits of labour-saving strategies. More important, though, is that the concept of productivity now emphasizes such factors as quality, ability to handle variations of the same product, and change-over times, as opposed to the traditional Taylorist factor of quantity per measure of labour input (Gustavsen 1986). Such a shift in emphasis logically (but not inevitably) leads to a changed relationship between management and labour. For example, Abernathy, Clark, and Kantrow (1983) point out that the Japanese built their automobile industry on the basis of quality, while the United States built its on the basis of minimizing costs. Consequently, their approach to labour is quite different: 'Americans buy and sell labour and the Japanese build a production process around it' (79). A skilled and committed workforce can make a significant difference in the achievement of such productivity concepts as quality.

In addition, Pava (1986a) argues that the inherent nature of advanced information systems technology severs the link between output and hours of labour. It thereby 'nullifies' the traditional view of labour as an incremental commodity. Instead, labour is seen as 'adding a competitive edge' rather than as a cost to be minimized. Similarly, a recent OECD (1986) study of the service sector states that 'Capital in the form of computers amplifies rather than displaces labour, so that workers act more intelligently' (4). The study goes on to state that in a post-industrial world productivity increases by 'increasing the quality of labour and capital, while more effectively co-ordinating their interaction' (2). The new paradigm, then, calls into question the basic relationship between labour and management, including assumptions about the nature of conflict.

Regulation by Rules

The proposition that the best way to regulate behaviour is through rules is deeply imbedded in society. 'Where law ends, tyranny begins,' proclaims the stone inscription on the United States Hall of Justice in Washington. (Law, according to the *Concise Oxford Dictionary*, is a binding set of rules.) For unions, the adoption of the rule-based approach to regulation has its roots in union struggles to limit the tyrannical rule of first line supervisors. However, this mechanical approach to regulation facilitated the development of scientific management, weakened some traditional union bases for power, and has become such a fundamental and well-developed component of collective bargaining that its limitations threaten unions' (and managements') ability to come to grips with new forms of work organization.

Prior to the triumph of the technocratic bureaucracy, foremen were a cross between straw bosses and contractors. Management delegated to foremen the power to hire, fire, and direct, and turned a blind eye when these foremen established highly personal labour markets. Foremen commonly hired and promoted according to ethnic prejudices, bribes, and family relationships, and created havoc and resentment with their often tyrannical exercise of power. Industrial unions played a major rule in finally disciplining foremen, subjecting them to standardized rules governing pay and promotion, and keeping a watchful eye on their every move through the grievance procedure. In that way, unions effected a virtual revolution in plant relations. Unions reduced the status of foremen from junior partners of management to junior management police (Roberts 1984).

However, the tyrannical foreman was also an obstacle to the effective and rational organization of the enterprise (Salaman 1981). As long as foremen's powers were unchecked, it was impossible fully to develop the scientific management paradigm. Of what use was it to have time and motion studies if supervisors assigned rates on the basis of personal preferences? Scientific management substituted 'the government of fact and law for the rule of force and opinion. It substitutes exact knowledge for guesswork and seeks to establish a code of natural laws equally binding upon employers and workmen' (Taylor 1911). Just as new forms of work organization are a threat to the foremen of today (Klein 1984), scientific management was a threat to the foremen of yesterday.

In addition to hastening the development of scientific management, in the process of dismantling the foremen's source of arbitrary power, unions also reduced some of their own power to take direct action in their interests. As foremen lost managerial discretion, union stewards also lost some discretion to pursue goals immediately (Lichtenstein 1982; Nash 1983). Instead, stewards became policemen of the agreement – the book or set of rules. Furthermore, the 'slack' in scientific management that gave foremen their formidable powers also gave certain strategically located work groups – the kill room in packing plants, the tirebuilders in rubber plants, and the sheetmill men in steel plants – power to seek improvements in direct but informal ways. These ways, labelled as continuous, fractional bargaining (Kuhn 1961), were sharply curtailed, though not eliminated, by the development of the rule-based approach to regulation. (The involvement of fractions or interest groups in collective bargaining in the new paradigm of organization will be explored in some detail in the analysis of the ECWU local 800's case.)

The successful fit between rule-based regulation and the early needs of unions and scientific management quickly led to their unquestioned acceptance as *the* mode of regulating the relation between union and management. The detailed and comprehensive nature of plant level agreements (i.e., rules) that govern the various aspects of work organization is a hallmark of the American collective bargaining scene (Kochan and Katz 1983). According to Roberts (1984), collective bargaining with its statutes (the agreement), its common law (arbitration decision), and its judiciary (arbitrators) can be likened to a legal or rule-based system. While rules, especially in the form of laws, are intended to reflect ideals (e.g., justice) they often constitute the routinized means of applying the dominant ideology (e.g., scientific management) to particular situations and reduce the area for debate (Clegg 1983). The following story from a United Steel Workers of America (USWA) publication used in the training of its officials makes just this point. A union member complained about the injustice of an arbitrator's decision. His lawyer cut him off with the reminder: 'justice has noting to do with it, the law is what determines the decisions' (Montgomery 1966).

However, in today's turbulent environment, rules are not a sufficient form of regulation; ideals are essential (Emery 1977). The levels of complexity, interdependence, and uncertainty found in turbulent environments are too high to be regulated by rules. Rules are better suited to dealing with issues which are easily quantifiable and involve a straightforward cause-and-effect relation. As will be discussed in detail later, rules are dysfunctional in dealing with many of the issues central to the design of new forms of work organization. These include designing roles to enable workers to learn continuously or working through the allocation of responsibilities between a semi-autonomous work group and the rest of the organization. Moreover, these issues are not peripheral to the development of more effective organizations: they are the heart of the issue. Unions therefore must develop an alternative to the rules approach in order to regulate developments that are too far-reaching and complex to be handled solely by rules.

Each of the five factors described above significantly shapes the substance and form of industrial unionism and its approach to collective bargaining. However, the full extent of their influence can only be seen when these factors are viewed as a system whose parts reinforce each other and whose sum effect defines a paradigm of union policy and practice. In this paradigm, which exists within, reflects and reinforces, the larger paradigm of scientific management, each factor performs a different but related function. The view that all conflict is distributive conflict is the key premise. Given this premise (and the objective conditions of Taylorism) job control is a logical key strategy for achieving job and income security. Furthermore, rules are well suited as the administrative method for dealing with distributive conflict and for making concrete the strategy of job control. Solidarity is critical in the win-lose struggle with management; therefore, uniformity, the easiest and perhaps the only basis for such solidarity in the disconnected world of scientific management, became a broadly accepted union norm. Finally, an unintended but inevitable consequence of this system is the exacerbation of the representative nature of unions. Representatives in turn are prone to using 'objective,' uniform rules for dealing with issues at a distance (Gustavsen 1981). The point here is not to explore what led to what, but to establish that the five key factors are tightly integrated. This can be illustrated by examining the link between rules and the other four components of the system.

The legal or rule-based administrative system that pervades collective bargaining grew out of the adversary relationship between labour and management. Detailed, legalistic contracts are a reaction to the principle of management rights. Since every function not specified, limited, or restricted in the agreement belongs to management, unions set out to specify, limit, and restrict. From the union's point of view, the goal is to straight-jacket management (Forrest 1978). Rules were and are well suited to achieving this goal. In fact, since the union is in a subordinate power position vis-à-vis management it will strive for a maximum of rules in order to protect itself. Management, on the other hand, will push rules only to a certain point (Gustavsen 1981). This point will make the union's behaviour predictable and possible and management's somewhere between predictable and random, thus maintaining and enhancing its superior power position. However, from management's point of view, it is also important to hold the line on union inroads into management rights. Hence, management as well sets out to specify, limit, and restrict. Contracts (often hundreds of pages long) are therefore written in precise rules which clearly spell out gains and losses. Such precision is in the interests of both parties.

The idea that rules are well suited to regulating distributive conflict is perhaps best illustrated by this story attributed to George Harris, a negotiator for the United Electrical Workers Union (UE) in the 1940s: 'Three longshoremen were bragging to a UE member about their contract, saying "it has lots of 'ums-minimums, all sorts of 'ums. How many 'ums you got in your contract?" the longshoreman asked. "Just one," replied the UE stalwart, "Fuck 'um!" ' (Roberts 1984).

The excessive use of rules, in turn, contributes to excessive reliance on experts, so characteristic of the representative nature of unions. Once management began winning more and more arbitration cases by hiring lawyers, unions soon responded in kind (Montgomery 1966). As a result, members are often not involved in handling their own disputes. However, reliance on lawyers further reinforced the use of precise detailed rules which forsake general principles for the concrete coverage of 'all' possible situations (the principle of total specification). 'No weasel wording' states a USWA handbook on negotiations; 'Remember, lawyers make their living from finding loopholes in laws written by other lawyers and all make a good living at it' (Montgomery 1966).

Rules are also especially effective in establishing the uniform job hierarchies and strict demarcations that characterize scientific management. They enhance union control over rates of pay and allow a basis for demands of equal pay for equal work and promotion on the basis of objective, measurable criteria. The drive for job control through the rules received its fullest expression in the Co-operative Wage Study Programme (CWS) developed by the USWA. Prior to CWS, the basic steel industry was marked by wage disparities from region to region, mill to mill, and person to person. It was to neither party's advantage to endure the friction and resentment created by these differentials. Instead, at the union's instigation, both union and management created a rule-based rating system, weighted to skill and responsibility but also taking account of effort and working conditions. This would ensure, the union claimed, that the 'basic rate for each job depends not on the personality or sex of the worker, nor, as in some cases, on the whim of the foreman or plant superintendent, but on the job' (Steelworker 1955). Both parties had a vested interest in a uniform objective, impersonal coding system, and both parties used industrial engineers. Neither suggested redesigning the job structure to create jobs with challenge, autonomy, and skill. The framework for CWS was set by scientific management (Roberts 1984).

Finally, rules were an effective means for making concrete the principle of solidarity through uniformity. There can be no debate about 'special treatment' when there is no doubt about the criterion.

A review of industrial relations literature reveals a consistent uneasiness about the fit between collective bargaining in general and industrial unionism in particular and the characteristics of the emerging socio-economic environment. Harry Arthurs, a leading Canadian legal scholar, in his address at the opening of the University of Toronto's Centre for Industrial Relations, questioned whether the legal framework of labour relations was adapted to the transformations of the 1960s: 'Technology changes quickly, yet the parties often freeze their relationships in a collective agreement binding for two or three years and cannot legally sign an agreement for less than one ... our law of labour relations embodies the old expectations, the morality of the 1930's and 40's. No more is demanded than a minimal and murky statutory duty to 'bargain in good faith" and adherence to a judicially drafted set of Marquis of Queensbury rules for industrial warfare ... the challenge for men of law is to avoid the collision of irresistible social forces and immovable legal objects' (Arthurs 1966, 93).

H.D. Woods, chairman of the influential Canadian federal task force that surveyed the violent picket line confrontations and alienation of union members from leaders that became hallmarks of the mid-1960s strike wave, was more direct. While paying tribute to the democratic achievements of unions and the collective bargaining systems, namely curbing or elimination of arbitrary authority in the hands of management, he also drew attention to the serious problems that remained.

Workers who have long resented their terms and conditions of employment and management's authority over them now seem to be reacting to an even more basic grievance. An increasing number of workers appear to perceive an issue in the nature of their jobs and perhaps in the very idea of work as it is now structured, whereby people were turned into little more than appendages to machines, denied self discipline, discretion and responsibility ... unions, like management, have failed in this new and more challenging area, and to some extent this failure is due to the fact that unions and the collective bargaining process were not designed to handle problems growing out of the nature of work itself. It is debatable whether the process could rise appropriately to the challenge. Indeed, under some circumstances unions, if not collective bargaining itself, might prove a hindrance. (Woods 1969, 94).

These conjectures by Arthurs and Woods have stood the test of time. There is an irrevocable incompatibility between industrial unionism and the emerging paradigm of organization. Ironically, in their success in limiting the destructiveness of scientific management, industrial unions themselves have come to embody its very essence. For example, the senior legal counsel for the United Steelworkers of America told a conference of arbitrators in 1956 that exclusive management rights merely recognize 'that somebody must be boss ... People can't be wandering around at loose ends, each deciding what to do next ... to assure order, there is a clear procedural line drawn: the company directs, the union grieves, when it objects' (Goldberg 1973). Frederick Taylor could not have said it better.

Craft Unionism

The rise of scientific management at the turn of the century was associated with the explusion of craft unions from heavy industry. Management, therefore, exercised unilateral power for several decades until industrial unionism triumphed in the 1930s and 1940s. By this time, the basic percepts of scientific management, the separation of thinking from doing, fractionated jobs, and a hierarchy of control, were a fait accompli. The industrial unions were unable to challenge this old paradigm of organization. Indeed, as I have argued, in their attempts to limit its destructiveness they both reinforced and incorporated its very essence. For some, the policies and practices of industrial unionism were widely accepted as *the* approach to unionism. A brief review of union policy and practice prior to the era of scientific management, the era of the craft union, demonstrates that an alternative has at least existed in the past. For a more detailed discussion, from a labour perspective, of the characteristics and evolution of craft (and industrial) unions the reader is referred to Heron (1989) and Heckscher (1988). A management view can be found in Lawrence (1985).

Before the development of scientific management, collective bargaining was barely practised. Instead, what Chamberlain (1945) called the precursor to collective bargaining, unilateral coercion, was the norm. The following descriptions of this norm are based upon Roberts's 1984 summary of his 1978 study of Toronto area unions in the period 1890–1914 and Stone's (1975) study of the American steel industry. Both studies treat craft unions in a favourable light. However, Jacoby (1984) points out some of the shortcomings of craft unions. These include the difficulties immigrant workers faced in progressing from helpers to journeymen.

According to Roberts, unions developed their demands, passed them at conventions, established them in their constitutions and rulebooks, and simply enforced them unilaterally. These demands usually covered rates of pay, standards of a fair day's work (the origin of the strategy of job control), rules on the rates of apprentices to journeymen, and the like – a host of pay and control issues that led employers to complain about 'union dictation.' In certain trades, supervisors were not allowed in work areas, lest they insult the integrity of proud tradesmen; in other trades, foremen were union members and subject to union discipline.

The taproot of this 'bargaining' power was the craft mastery possessed by the artisan, and by the artisan alone.

In the days when moulders were 'sand artists,' when machinists were engineers, and construction workers doubled as architects, the mysteries of a trade and its undocumented rules of thumb gave the monopoly of production knowledge to workers. Shop rules were shaped by the same rules of thumb. Whatever agreements were signed had no status in law until the 1940's. Indeed, the fiercely individualistic artisans rarely relied on the force of law, preferring the force of their own self-reliance, self-discipline and solidarity based on loyalty to a vocation. Unions provided unemployment, sickness and death benefits. They were, as almost all the unions of the epoch titled themselves, 'brotherhoods.' (Roberts 1984, 40)

In both cases, the basis for this pre-scientific management mode of unionism was the craftsmen's monopoly over the knowledge necessary for production. The few trades (e.g., construction and garment workers) which still enjoy this monopoly today continue to practise a version of the 'dated' style of unionism and collective bargaining. According to Piore and Sabel (1984), 'Many features of shop-floor control in construction and garment making reflect the peculiarities of those industries. Yet the critical elements of both are typical of the craft sector in general: the link between wages and skill; the control of short-term job-security through work sharing; the defense of long-term job security through monopolization of skill; and collaboration between labour and management in the organization of work' (119). These anachronisms are, however, the exception that proves the rule. The ascendancy of scientific management virtually spelled the end of this form of unionism. The industrial form which replaced it could not rely on control over the supply of skilled labour, the solidarity bred by loyalty to a craft vocation, or the unwritten 'laws' of a trade to achieve its goals. Instead, as I have argued, industrial unionism developed a form suited to its environment. As this environment now rapidly changes, the challenge is to develop still another form of unionism.

Stone's history of the American steel industry paints a similar picture.

In the 19th century, work in the steel industry was controlled by the skilled workers and their union, the Amalgamated Association of Iron, Steel and Tin Workers, the strongest union of its time. The workers and their union decided how the work was done and how much was produced. Owners and managers played a very small role in production and there were few foremen. The workers, like their counterparts in the iron industry, contracted with the steel companies to produce steel. In this labour system, there were two types of workers, skilled and unskilled. Skilled workers did work that required training, experience, dexterity and judgment. The selection, training and promotion of future skilled workers was controlled by the craftsmen and their union. Unskilled workers performed the heavy manual labour, some were hired directly by the company, others by the skilled workers. Steel was made by teams of skilled workers and unskilled helpers who controlled the pace of work and division of labour and who used the companies' equipment and raw material. Workers were paid a certain sum, a tonnage rate, for each ton of steel they produced. The union negotiated a sliding scale with the owners which made the tonnage rate fluctuate with the market price of steel and iron. The workers, in the context of their union, decided on how to divide up the tonnage rate among themselves. (Stone 1975, 60)

According to Griffin, Wallace, and Rubin (1986) the craftworkers' near monopoly of knowledge about the production process enabled them ... to be free of supervision, to pace their own work, and to produce at an output quota fixed by the workers themselves' (150). Similarly, John Fitch (quoted in Stone 1975), a journalist who had interviewed hundreds of steelworkers and steel officials for his history of the steelworkers, concluded that in some steel mills, 'the men ran the mill' (32). Not surprisingly, the famous Homestead strike, a landmark in the struggle between management and craft unions over the introduction of scientific management, took place in a steel mill.

2 New Forms of Work Organization and the Union Response

Five points stand out when one reviews the last ten to fifteen years of union experience in grappling with new forms of work organization. First, there has been a noticeable increase in the number of unions involved in organization redesign projects. Second, there are considerable differences among unions in their views concerning the value and function of these new organizational forms. Third, the two approaches followed by unions in response to the strategic issue of integrating these new forms and contract negotiation and administration are fundamentally flawed. Fourth, at the level of the primary work system (Trist 1981), the types of innovation with which unions have been associated do not strongly embody the principles of the new paradigm of organization. Furthermore, the settings in which these innovations occur do not 'naturally' favour the development of the paradigm. Finally, there has been very little research examining the effect of the new forms of work organization on unions. This chapter elaborates each of the five points.

Extent of Union Involvement

In the late 1960s and early 1970s, projects aimed at designing or redesigning the workplace were undertaken, with rare exceptions, in non-union settings. One reason behind the low level of union involvement is succinctly captured in this 1970 statement by William Winpisinger, international president of the International Association of Machinists (IAM): 'If you want to enrich the job, enrich the paycheque.' By 1986, however, the situation had changed. In Canada, the Canadian Autoworkers Union (CAW), the United Steelworkers of America (USWA), the Energy and Chemical Workers Union (ECWU), the United Food and Commercial Workers (UFCW), the Public Service Alliance of Canada (PSAC), the Ontario Public Service Employees Union (OPSEU), and the International Woodworkers of America (IWA) have all had locals involved in some sort of work redesign projects. Some have developed policies to assist locals. In the United States, the UAW, the USWA, the IUE, and the CWA have signed national agreements with their respective employers which call for the development of joint union-management projects. The UAW and General Motors alone have projects in over 80 plants. Even the IAM in both countries has participated in several projects. The reasons behind this growth in union involvement include the visionary leadership of a few senior union officials, such as Neil Reimer of the ECWU and Irving Bluestone of the UAW, and the desire to retain jobs in the face of increased and often international competition.[1]

Union Views

Increased union participation in developing new forms of work organization has been accompanied by considerable controversy within the union movement. Three positions can be identified. The first, as represented by the ECWU in Canada and the UAW in the United States, argues that unions must take the lead in developing new forms of work organization (Reimer 1979; Bluestone 1982). Proponents of this position initiate work redesign projects. They believe that union objectives in both traditional and innovative work settings are essentially the same – enhanced human dignity and restriction of managerial autocracy. What is different is that the new work forms enlarge the arena of union influence. These positions are often supported by official policies and the development of internal expertise in the area of work design.

The second, and in Canada the predominant, position, as represented by the United Electrical Workers, UE (1984), and by the Canadian Union of Public Employees, CUPE (Stinson 1982), argues that QWL, the quality of working life, is at best a productivity gimmick.[2] When stripped of its rhetoric about ongoing communication and direct employee involvement, QWL's real purpose is revealed: 'to weaken worker reliance on the collective agreement and their union' (Stinson 1982). Proponents of this position actively campaign against union involvement in work redesign projects.

The third position, which is usually not spelled out in a policy document, is ambivalent about new forms of work organization. According to this position, only careful 'experimentation' will provide the evidence necessary to take an unequivocal position. In practice, this position of ambivalent 'neutrality' often results in local unions having to cope on their own with requests for participation in work design projects from local managements fully supported by their head offices.

The three views discussed above are consistent with a recent study of national union representatives' views of worker participation in the United States (Kochan, Katz, and Mower 1984). This study found a continuum of views ranging from general opposition to decentralized neutrality to decentralized policy with national union support to general endorsement.

Contract Negotiation and Administration

Unions, in working with management to develop new forms of work organization, have had to deal with the strategic question of how to relate these new forms to contract negotiations and administration. Two approaches have been developed. The first, and most prevalent, with the exception of letters of intent and general guide-lines, rigidly separates one from the other. The second attempts to accommodate new forms of work organization through, and without changing, the traditional system of contract negotiation and administration.'[3] Both strategies are fundamentally flawed as they reflect a limited understanding of the new organizational paradigm and ignore the systemic nature of organizations, especially the interdependence between job and organization design and collective bargaining. In fact, the first approach explains, in part, the high number of change projects which do not survive beyond two to three years.

The separation approach has proved a useful formulation for

providing many unions with the political protection and psychological comfort necessary to participate in the development of new forms of organization. The UAW (Bluestone 1977) is the probable originator and best-known advocate of this strategy, which has been adopted by several major unions (e.g., USWA [Camens 1983] and CWA [Watts 1982]). In practice, this approach has meant that all issues covered by the contract are strictly off limits to the development process. However, since collective agreements typically cover such issues as job classifications, pay, and seniority, fundamental aspects of the workplace (e.g., the design of jobs) are ignored.

The separation approach is usually part of the transitional model (Walton 1984) for shifting existing organizations from the old to the new paradigm. However, at best this model is a temporary equilibrium between the two. Just how temporary can be seen in the number of change projects in existing organizations (roughly 45 per cent) which do not survive beyond two or three years (Mansell 1983). Ironically, union strategy in these projects has contributed to this high attrition rate.

While the separation of new forms of work organization and contract negotiation and administration may have been politically and psychologically useful, it is perhaps best described as a convenient fiction. Every change project worth its salt has strayed into issues covered by the contract. Many of the reasons for these 'transgressions' often have little to do with management's desire to bypass the union and 'negotiate' directly with the workers. Nor have they to do with union ploys of 'going shopping' for what couldn't be won at the bargaining table. Instead, the overlap between the two processes is a logical and inevitable outcome of a mature change process and the systemic nature of organizations.

Developing more flexible, participative organizations is, of course, possible without altering the contract. However, the degree of improvement, especially from a sts perspective, is significantly limited as long as the collective agreement is out of bounds. This is because certain contract clauses – for instance, those dealing with work rules (especially concerning the design of jobs which are standard features of most collective agreements – have a direct bearing on both organization flexibility and worker participation.

As the change process or new organizaition matures, it inevitably attempts to deal with these clauses. Katz (1985), in chapter 7 of his book on the transformation of the U.S. auto industry, nicely captures this tendency and the associated tensions and difficulties.

It is not a question of whether the two 'separate' processes of work organization and contract negotiation will collide, but of when. In industries where strong unions have negotiated elaborate contracts (e.g. automobile), it is sooner rather than later. In the public sector, with its more recently formed unions and more restricted bargaining scope, the collision is delayed but not avoided. Moreover, the systemic nature of organizations also contributed to the overlap between the two ostensibly separate processes.

Organizations are systems of interdependent parts. Consequently, the 'goodness' of the fit (Galbraith 1977; Galbraith and Nathanson 1978) or congruence among the parts is an important factor in determining overall effectiveness. Some items (e.g., progression systems) currently covered in most collective agreements are better suited to the ongoing, open problem-solving negotiations involved in the development of new forms of work organizations than to the periodic, close-to-the-vest trade-off negotiations of the contract. Not surprisingly, these items tend to gravitate to the former. The idea of the fit between the nature of issues and the processes for handling them will be explored in detail in chapter 4 in the description and analysis of the ECWU local 800 case.

When the inevitable spillover between the development of new forms of work organization and the collective agreement occurs, it frequently results in either the slow and quiet, or quick and noisy, termination of the change project. The scenario is usually as follows. The initial signs of the spillover are first noticed by low-level union and management officials who hasten to correct the 'problem' while concealing its existence from their superiors who are usually members of the joint steering committee overseeing the project. Efforts aimed at concealment prove futile and the steering committee inevitably becomes aware of the situation. Their diagnosis is almost always that a 'communication problem' exists and their response is to restate the project rules and disseminate them through further training. At this point the project either withers away, unable to survive on what is left over from the bargaining table, or explodes when either union or management (usually the former) interprets the spillover as an attempt by the other party to undermine the agreement. This scenario is becoming more and more common. For example, several CAW locals in Canada and the United States have recently voted to withdraw from worker-involvement projects. Ronchi and Morgan's (1981) analysis of the Columbus, Ohio, QWL program reveals a similar dynamic.

In private, some union officials (especially those at the local level) who are advocates of 'separation' will acknowledge that in certain circumstances a QWL/EI process has modified, and should be allowed to modify, the collective agreement. Such was the case in two UAW-GM projects at Livonia, at the Cadillac engine plant, and at the Delco Remy spark-plug plant in Georgia. To the author's knowledge the first North American project which explicitly altered the collective agreement to meet the requirements of developing a new form of work organization was the Rushton/United Mine Workers project (Trist, Susman, and Brown 1977). Modifying the collective agreement, however, is a long way from integrating new forms of work organization with contract negotiation and adminis-tration. Early reports suggest that such an integration is being developed in the GM/UAW Saturn project (Toronto Star, 3 August 1985). This dramatic development is consistent with Shell ECWU local 800's collective bargaining system.

Despite its limitations the strategy of separating contract negoti-ation and administration from the development of new forms of work organization at least acknowledges that the former is ill-suited to dealing with the latter. The innovative, if problematic nature of these new forms is not denied. However, the approach of accommodating these new forms within an unchanged collective bargaining system completely misses the point concerning what these new forms of work organization are all about. For example, Barbash (1977) claims that collective bargaining is already advanc-ing QWL by humanizing seniority and grievance procedures. And Lewin (1981) argues that 'collective bargaining is fundamentally a participative process and to propose that QWL can't be achieved through it is untenable, even ludicrous.' To a large degree these statements are true – at least in the context of scientific management.

The extent of the misreading of the nature of the new paradigm and its challenge to unions, by those who advocate a more-of-the-same approach, is perhaps best reflected in this recent statement by William Winpisinger, president of the IAM: 'where there are real problems, we will work with management through the already existing structure of inplant union representatives (i.e., local lodge officers, shop stewards, etc.). Why do we need some new organization when one already exists to handle these matters of mutual concern?' (quoted in Kochan, Katz, and Mower 1984, 66).

Both approaches to linking new forms of organization to contract negotiation and administration fail to come to grips with the new paradigm. The first forces the union into the, at best, awkward position of protecting traditional positions (e.g., job control) while promoting change (Brossard 1981). While allowing some direct representation in a restricted set of issues, acknowledging non-distributive conflict, and engaging in somewhat less legalistic rule-making, it is a strategy of piecemeal reform rather than system transformation. The separation approach has also led to an undue emphasis in the development of new forms of work organization on union management co-operation. In some cases, the rigid separation of contract negotiation and administration and the organization change process has left the latter so devoid of content that one aspect of the process – co-operation or jointness – has become equated or confused (van Beinum 1984) with the new paradigm itself. Ironically, in some situations, under the guise of QWL/EI, union and management have co-operated in 'fine-tuning' Taylorism.

The second approach to linking new forms of work organization and the contract puts the union in a position of a defender of the status quo. However, this approach will become more and more untenable as organizational flexibility is widely accepted as a legitimate management concern. Indeed, as Gustavsen (1986) argues, 'The slowness of many unions to develop a new type of strategy has provided powerful ammunition for those politicians, employers and managers who would gladly do without a strong trade union movement' (380).

Innovations and Their Settings

The fourth point which stands out in assessing union experience with new forms of work organization concerns the nature and setting of the various innovations. Much as been learned over the past twenty years about these aspects of development of the paradigm of organization. For purposes of this section four points are relevant. First, at the level of the primary work system, autonomous groups (Herbst 1962) most strongly embody the essence of the paradigm. Second, the more comprehensive the scope of the design the more complete is the elaboration of the paradigm and the more likely its long-term survival. The best setting, then, would seem to be the whole organization. Third, continuous process technologies appear to 'favour' the development of the paradigm. Finally, its most powerful illustrations to date are in new rather than existing organizations.

In cases involving unions, few innovations have involved autonomous groups. Most have been in settings ill-suited to developing and sustaining the paradigm fully. Projects for the most part have been concerned with the development of quality circles (Brunet 1981) or labour-management committees (Batt and Weinberg 1978) within parts of established organizations that use fabrication and assembly technologies.

The Primary Work System

At the level of the primary work system, autonomous groups, job enrichment (Herzberg, Mausner, and Snyderman 1959), and parallel structures (Stein and Kanter 1980; Herrick 1985) are the most common forms of innovation associated with the new paradigm of organization. The comparison which follows demonstrates that autonomous groups are by far the strongest embodiment of the paradigm.

Job enrichment is a very weak illustration of the new paradigm. It involves a number of different kinds and levels of tasks being added to the job to make it a more complete whole. Though concerned with socio-technical relations, it focuses on the individual job rather than the work system. In fact, some of its proponents

(Myers 1970; Ford 1969) foster the belief that shop and office-floor jobs can be designed without affecting the role of the supervisor. In this orthodox form it does not involve participation, but relies on experts brought in by management (Trist 1981).

Parallel structures are currently the most popular form of workplace innovation. The following discussion of parallel structures is taken from Mansell (1987a). The parallel-structure approach to developing new forms of work organization is characterized by the creation of a separate set of structures (e.g., committees, problem-solving groups) parallel to the primary organization structures, as a vehicle for more widespread participation, especially of the union and/or employees. It encompasses a number of similar approaches under different labels, including quality circles (QC), employee involvement (EI), many of the joint committees that go under the QWL label, and a variety of different problem-solving groups (e.g., within Scanlon Plans, preventative mediation programs, etc.).

In most cases, the parallel-structure approach involves setting up a two-tiered system of joint union/management committees. There is normally a plant or office-wide steering committee and several department or area committees. The steering committee is usually composed of several senior managers and the local union executive. Typically, the role of the steering committee is to oversee the operation of the area/department committees and to deal with plant/office-wide issues. The 'lower' level committees are almost always completely voluntary – no area/department need have a committee and no individual (with the exception of first-level supervisors) need participate. They are usually composed of eight to twelve workers, often assisted by a facilitator, and generally meet regularly (e.g., two hours a week).

Most area/department committees deal primarily with issues related to immediate working conditions, productivity, product quality, and health and safety. Committees are usually given some form of special training in conducting meetings and problem resolution, sometimes at a fairly sophisticated level.

Regardless of their label, all parallel structures coexist with, yet – in terms of flexibility and employee participation – contradict a generally traditional basic organization structure. Although the approach is most prevalent in redesign situations, it is also common in many new designs where either management or union, or both, are not prepared to venture too far with change. In this regard, it is interesting to note that in Japan quality circles do not contradict but are rather a consistent extension of a work organization characterized, in the primary labour market, by job rotation, skill development, and group work (Bradley and Hill 1983).

Despite some often impressive outcomes (e.g., Mansell 1987a), there are serious limitations to the parallel-structure approach to new forms of work organization. Ironically, but not surprisingly, some of the same characteristics of parallel structures that make them attractive are ultimately their weakness. The first and most obvious problem is the very fact that they are parallel. Since creating a parallel structure leaves the basic organization structure intact, it is relatively easy both to set up the additional structure and to dismantle it. Given this reality, it is quite possible for a parallel structure to be dismantled regardless of what might be happening within the change program itself. For example, many a parallel structure has died as the result of personnel changes in management or political events within the union, both at and beyond the local level.

The second major limitation inherent in parallel structures is less obvious, but more fundamental. One of the main reasons why parallel structures are so popular is that they are relatively unthreatening, since they are *not* set up to change the core traditions of either management or union. Although, theoretically, participation groups could work toward making more basic changes to existing structures, in practice they usually cannot because of both their mandate and their structure. Most QWL, EI, and problem-solving groups are not permitted to deal with issues related to corporate policy, basic management systems (e.g., the role of the engineering department), or the collective agreement. In addition, since most activity within parallel structures occurs at the area level, participation groups rarely have the resources to deal with, or often even to identify, many such organization-wide issues, even if they are not off-limits.

In practice, what this means is that once the groups have dealt with obvious problems and inefficiencies in their area, they hit a wall. Often, they want to begin addressing broader issues (related, for example, to hours of work, job classifications, the scope of managerial authority, etc.), but are called back 'in line' by management and/or the union. It is very common about two years into a parallel structure program for groups to complain that they are 'stuck,' that they have 'plateaued out.' Not surprisingly, the situation is even more frustrating for people when there is a gain-sharing component built into the program.

The lesson from ten years of experience with parallel structures is clear. Parallel structures can be a powerful approach for dealing with many issues. However, there are distinct limits to how far such programs can go. If, as this author believes, more fundamental organization change is required, then a different approach must be followed. Lawler and Mohrman (1985) reach a similar conclusion in their study of one type of parallel system – quality circles. They recommend that organizations seriously interested in participation should start with the development of natural work teams (i.e., autonomous groups).

By contrast, autonomous groups are a powerful illustration of the development of the new paradigm at the level of the primary work system. Autonomous work groups are teams of workers who have collective responsibility for an integrated set of tasks and who have considerable autonomous decision-making powers in relation to this more whole unit of work. It is important to note that autonomous groups are *not* defined in terms of the amount of social interaction between members, nor in the degree of multi-skilling among members. As Herbst (1985) points out, 'The essential characteristic of a group ... is [the] ... conjoint management of task interdependences' (23). According to Trist (1981):

Autonomous groups are learning systems. As their capabilities increase, they extend their decision space. In production units they tend to absorb certain maintenance and control functions. They become able to set their own machines. The problem-solving capability increases on day-to-day issues. They negotiate for their special needs with their supply and user departments. As time goes on, more of their members acquire more of the relevant skills. Yet most such groups allow a considerable range of preferences as regards multi-skilling and job interchange. The less venturesome and more modestly endowed can find suitable niches. The overall gain in flexibility can become very considerable, and this can be used to enhance performance and also to accommodate personal needs as regards time off, shifts, vacations, etc. (34)

There are, of course, cases where even limited multi-skilling or job interchange is not possible because of the complexity of the particular skills (e.g., a research and development department).[4] The group, however, still controls its own internal regulation.

The effectiveness of autonomous work groups is based largely on the cybernetic concept of self-regulation. 'The more key disturbances can be controlled directly by the group, the quicker the responses, the better the results and the higher member satisfaction. Over a wide array of situations the range of disturbances controllable by an autonomous groups is greater than that controllable by individuals separately linked to an external supervisor' (Trist 1981, 34). When the group is self-regulating the function of supervision is to manage the boundary conditions in the group's environment so that the group itself may be freed to manage its own activities.

One other innovation at the primary work system level not included in this comparison is network clusters (Herbst 1974, 1976). It, too, strongly embodies the principle of the new paradigm. However, insufficient application and research precludes its examination here. For a recent discussion of the emerging relevance of this organizational form the reader is referred to Pava (1983).

Scope of Design

In order both to elaborate the features of the new paradigm and to foster its survival, the unit of design must be a whole organization. This requires that the design encompass a primary work system (Trist 1981) and include an organization's support systems. A primary work system has a semi-independent operational identity and in unionized settings usually, but not necessarily, includes an entire bargaining unit. If the unit of design is not at least a primary work system, it will tend to become encapsulated and regress in the direction of the traditional paradigm (Hill 1971; Walton 1975).

Every organization has a range of systems, formal and informal, which support its basic values and goals by making sure that everything is working as it should. For example, there are systems for hiring employees, for providing orientation and training (both social and technical), for ensuring that people behave in a manner consistent with the organization's goals, for allocating resources (money, materials, people), and for handling the relationship between union and management. In order for the new paradigm to develop and be sustained, it is essential that these support systems be adapted to fit the new values and goals reflected within the paradigm (Mansell and Rankin 1983).

Technology

Technology, of course, does not determine organization. Many different socio-technical systems, including those reflecting both Taylorist and new paradigm design principles, can operate a given technology. However, technology is not neutral (Lie 1983). The particular characteristics of any technology can be more or less supportive of a general form of work organization. For example, Herbst (1985) points out that technology determines the task structure and task relationships in any organization. These in turn constrain or facilitate – but do not determine – the possible allocation of people to tasks, a major but not the only component of the design of the entire work organization. Zuboff (1982) argues that the new computer-based technology, in addition to closing the simple information loops, increases skill levels by requiring greater analytical abilities on the part of operators. And Pava (1986) points out that new technologies can achieve levels of system integration so that an operator error can be transmitted virtually instantaneously throughout the entire system. Finally, Susman (1986) states that in a computer-integrated factory, communication patterns will be changed dramatically: ' ... lower level personnel will be as likely to initiate such exchanges with those at the upper levels as they are to receive them, and the horizontal flow of information across functions and manufacturing cells will also be reciprocal' (267).

'Good' technology, though, is not enough (Elden et al 1982). The design of any socio-technical system is the outcome of a complex pattern of interaction of a host of variables including market conditions, design competence, and the balance of power between union and management.

Continuous process technologies appear to 'favour' the development of the new paradigm. Until recently the autonomous group form of innovation has been found primarily, but by no means exclusively, in the petrochemical sector. (For an example of an autonomous work group in a government office involving routine clerical work, see Mansell [1987a].) The dominant technology in this sector is a highly automated, continuous process. The *effective* operation of continuous process technologies requires the formation of work groups with considerable autonomy (Mallet 1963; Taylor 1971; Emery 1980). Groups are required since output is the result of varied inputs of a number of workers. Individual contribution is difficult to assess. Autonomy is necessary since workers must respond almost instantaneously to unpredictable rather than predictable events (Davis 1983). The cost of an error can be quite high. A successful operation places a high premium on individual commitment to act when needed, the existence of an appropriate-response repertoires, and the delegation of authority.

Continuous process technologies also affect the kind of skills required by the workforce. Because of automation, direct intervention to control conversion uncertainties (e.g., temperature) (Susman 1976) is minimal. Workers are predominantly involved in controlling boundary transaction uncertainties (Susman 1986); that is, the planning, design, programming, and monitoring of the automated production processes. The skills associated with these tasks are those of the emerging, rather than the traditional, paradigm of organization. Indeed Pava (1986a) argues that 'knowledge-based contributions previously defined as tertiary – such as preventative maintenance, systems improvement, and training – will become an ongoing, everyday priority for maintaining a competitive advantage' (215). And Adler (1986) argues that in general new technology tends to upskill not de-skill tasks and that the emerging skill profile demands that workers exercise responsibility not just effort, be capable of abstract reasoning not just rote learning, and develop the social skills necessary for working effectively in highly integrated systems.[5] These are just the type of skills associated with continuous process technologies.

In the office sector (e.g., insurance companies) job enrichment, with its individual focus, has been the favoured form of innovation. This is because the nature of the interaction among workers handling office technologies has been assumed to be sequential (i.e., passing messages along the line) rather than interactive. Underlying this assumption is a vision of information as something which can be objectified and machine-bound (Gustavsen 1983a).

In the manufacturing sector, the size of investment in Tayloristic assembly and fabrication technologies (e.g., the assembly line), and hence the entrenched power of the industrial engineering function, has favoured the application of parallel structures. These do not directly attack existing powers nor do they require significant technological change (Heckscher 1980).

New Organizations

The elaboration and survival over time of the new paradigm is much more likely in new than in established organizations (Pava 1979; Walton 1980). As Trist (1981) argues, developing the paradigm in established organizations involves dealing with the 'accumulated practices of the past as well as accommodating an array of vested interests' (44). For example, Kochan, Katz, and McKersie (1986) point out that changes in existing work practices and rules can 'alter individual worker's status, employment security and promotion opportunities' (86). Even when union officials and management co-operate, the strength of workers' 'second line of defences' (e.g., on-the-job customs and procedures) is often too powerful to overcome (Emery 1980). In addition, the costs of making changes to the technical subsystem are often prohibitive. These constraints are lessened considerably in new organizations.

In many new organizations the opportunity to approach the ideal of joint optimization of the social and technical subsystems more closely can be realized. For example, according to the internal consultant, several technologies were considered in the design of Miracle Food Mart's Toronto meat-processing plant. A key criterion in assessing the appropriateness of the various technologies was their fit with the desired socio-technical system. Furthermore, new designs are almost always whole organizations in that they encompass both a primary work system and its accompanying support systems. Finally, the rare chance to 'build from scratch' often generates considerable commitment and creativity.

Union Experience

Most projects that have involved autonomous groups and have been undertaken in favourable settings (e.g. new plants) have been in non-union organizations (e.g., Lawler 1978). Management, in many cases, views these projects as a key strategy in remaining union-free (Poza 1983). Unions have been unsuccessful in organizing employees in these plants. To the writer's knowledge, only in one case (a GM plant) have employees in such projects been organized without the employer succumbing to threats of industrial action in already unionized sister plants or offices. In some cases, according to the director of the Northeast Labor Management Center in Boston, unionists have viewed such plants as being totally and irrevocably incompatible with unionism. Even in the case of General Motors, according to senior management and union officials, the UAW, until recently, has chosen not to be actively involved in the design of GM's new team-based plants.

Extent and Nature of Research

There is a growing awareness of the critical significance for unions of new forms of work organization. For example, Kochan and Katz (1983) state 'If these changes survive over time and diffuse to more settings, the character of the U.S. collective bargaining and industrial relations system at the plant level will be fundamentally altered ... these newer forms of organizations ... pose severe challenges for the local union.' The extent of the severity of these challenges is revealed in a two-and-a-half-year study on the state of the labour movement commissioned by the AFL-CIO. The study suggests that workplace innovations along the lines of the new paradigm are a key factor in the decline in United States union membership (List 1985). However, there has been little research examining the effect on unions of new forms of work organization. Existing research is mainly theoretical. With a few recent exceptions, field research has only touched on some aspects of the impact of new ways of organizing work on unions.

Theoretical research suggests that more flexibility in unions' traditional positions regarding promotion, job classification, and wage payment systems is necessary for the development of new forms of organization (Tchobanian 1975). However, as I have argued earlier, the legal underpinnings of the Canadian and American industrial relations systems discourage changes in these positions. Residual rights belong to management; unions are encouraged to exert as much specific control as possible over as many aspects of work life as permitted by law, by negotiating into a collective agreement a rigid web of rules, procedures, and definitions.

Certain field studies have touched upon the effect of the new organization paradigm on unions. An assessment of the Harman Industries/UAW project found both that the majority of union members felt the project strengthened the union and that members' satisfaction with their leadership was significantly higher than the national average (Macy 1980). *Business Week*, in a 1981 review of American developments, noted that all local union leaders involved in UAW/GM projects were re-elected. A cursory review of several projects concludes that substantial changes are required in both the theory and practice of collective bargaining to incorporate direct worker involvement (Schlesinger and Walton 1977). An earlier report of the ECWU/Shell experience (Davis and Sullivan 1980) contains a brief description of their collective agreement. Finally, a recent publication (Cohen-Rosenthal 1984) concludes that new forms of work organization increase member participation in the union, demand more leadership involvement with the membership and change the approach to resolving grievances.

These studies, while helpful, are incomplete. Either unions were not the focal point of the reports, or the studies were very preliminary in nature. However, recent reports from both the industrial relations (Kochan, Katz, and Mower 1984) and labour process literature (Wells 1987; Parker and Slaughter 1988) contain in-depth studies of the effect of new forms of work organization on unions.

The main empirical base for the industrial relations study's findings came from a survey of and interviews with over 100 union officers and 900 members in five different QWL programs. Despite some methodological weaknesses and the theoretical orientation of its authors, the study supports my conclusion that the new paradigm demands a fundamental transformation of unions, policies, and practices. Methodologically, the study suffers from its decision to include a wide range of innovations under the heading of worker participation. Four cases of weak manifestations of the new paradigm (i.e., quality circles, labour-management committees) are lumped together with only one strong one (i.e., autonomous work groups). While the data are sometimes broken down by type of innovation, the data concerning the views of local union officials on the effect of worker participation on the union are not.

The theoretical orientation of the authors is clearly evident in the opening and concluding chapters. The opening chapter traces, inaccurately in this writer's opinion, the theoretical underpinnings of the new paradigm to early human relations theory (Mayo 1946). References to the socio-technical school (e.g., Davis, Emery, and Trist) are conspicuous by their absence. Ironically, while the authors correctly castigate early proponents of QWL for largely ignoring the history of industrial relations and collective bargaining, they too ignore history. The absence of a sts perspective, though, does not prevent the authors from concluding that the new paradigm may represent a new industrial and human resources development policy. However, it does lead them, in the concluding chapter, incorrectly to limit the new paradigm to psychological issues, artificially to rank people's economic interests over their social/psychological dimensions, and to ignore the lessons from other countries (e.g., Norway, Sweden) for the development of industrial and human resources policies based on the new paradigm of organization. The consequences for unions of, and an alternative to, arranging members' 'bread and butter' economic interests and psychological needs in a hierarchy will be discussed in chapter 5, in my analysis of how local 800 is able to mobilize for collective action. In addition, I will draw upon relevant developments in the Scandinavian countries in order, in chapter 4, to analyse the Shell/local 800 collective bargaining system.

Despite these drawbacks the study supports my analysis of the mismatch between current union policy and practice and the new paradigm of organization. It found that new forms of work organization result in a shift away from the job-control form of unionism. It also found that these new forms challenge the union to integrate direct and indirect forms of representation, reduce the reliance on strict rules for governing jobs, and increase the variations in the use of human resources. These, in return, challenge unions' use of standardization for internal union control.

The comments of one respondent cited in the study vividly capture the depth of this challenge: 'I guess it depends on the definition of weakness and strength. If we look at the union as encouraging grievances and opposing management, if that's perceived as strength, then I would hope this process would weaken that. I think the role of the union might be strengthened if it evolves into something else, a new role. I'd hope to see lower decision making in the organization so that it will be flatter than it is now, one in which good employees would be given more time and recognition. Now the union is protecting the bad people. If we could take better care of the good, I'll be happy.'

The labour process studies are highly critical of the impact on unions of new forms of work organization. QWL, EI, etc., are seen as subtle control strategies which undermine worker solidarity and manipulate workers' minds and hearts so they pursue management goals even at the cost of their own jobs. Both studies conclude by exhorting unions to develop their own version of QWL, their own agenda for redesigning the workplace. This is just what ECWU local 800 has done – but in a manner which recognizes the changing nature of production and the resultant need for unions to alter some past practices and traditions.

3

The Shell Sarnia
Chemical Plant:
The Future
in the Present?

The question of how best to examine the relationship between unions and new forms of work organization demands that the researcher focus on one or a combination of levels of the union organization. There are several levels to chose from: local, district, national, international, and umbrella. I have chosen the local level for three reasons. First, new forms of work organization are developed at the level of the enterprise. Accordingly, their effect on unions should be most pronounced at the local level. Second, there is a growing awareness of the limitations of central bodies for understanding, let alone controlling, 'lower' level development, and of the need to rethink the relationship between centre and periphery (Schon 1971). In the case of unions the appropriate starting place for such a rethinking would seem to be a deeper appreciation of the complexities of local union developments. Finally, I have chosen the local level because, for the most part, Canadian and American unions, unlike some of their European counterparts, exercise power primarily at this level.

This chapter is divided into three sections. The first describes my research methodology – case study – and argues why it and my sample size (one) are appropriate for examining the relationship between unions and the emerging paradigm of organization. The second section provides background information on the Energy and Chemical Workers Union and describes in detail the organization design of the Shell chemical plant. The chapter concludes with a review of some of the concepts of negotiations theory which relate to my study of local 800.

Methodology

Case-study methodology is a form of social-science inquiry which attempts to examine, from a holistic standpoint, a contemporary phenomenon in its real-life context (Yin 1981). It assumes that human beings, far from merely responding to the social world, actively contribute to its development (Morgan and Smircich 1980). Case study is an especially appropriate method for opening a new field of study or breaking new ground (Emery 1963). The preliminary nature of existing research on the subject of unions and new forms of work organization has been discussed in chapter 2. Furthermore, my analysis of union's approach to linking the new forms of work organization and contract negotiation and administration shows that the current 'theories in use' (Argyris and Schon 1974) have reached an impasse.

The case-study method does not usually produce universally applicable generalizations. Findings are typically contingent upon the situation being studied. Generalizations can only be made on the basis of recurring patterns extracted from a number of cases (Diesing 1971). Because I am studying only one case and because there has been so little related research, my study is hypotheses-generating (Lijphart 1971) in nature. However, the significance of my findings is enhanced considerably by my choice of case. As Emery (1963) has argued, the value of the case method is in the selection of cases where 'we have reason to believe that the necessary and sufficient conditions for events may be most easily discovered or most easily verified.' Such conditions are present in the case of ECWU local 800. In chapter 2 I established that the settings most conducive to developing and sustaining the new paradigm are whole, new organizations utilizing continuous process technologies. These three features characterize the Shell Sarnia plant. Furthermore, the design of the plant (which is detailed later) follows the socio-technical design principles which underlie the new paradigm and includes autonomous work groups, the strongest embodiment of the paradigm at the level of the primary work system. In addition, the age of the plant (nine years from design, seven years from commissioning) and the length of my involvement (six years, three informally, three formally) allow me to trace the development of the new paradigm and the union over time. This is particularly important since different issues are salient at different stages in the development of a new work system (Mansell and Rankin 1983). Finally, and of critical importance, the ECWU has played an active, leading role in both the design and ongoing development of the Sarnia plant. In fact, this was a condition of their involvement (Halpern 1984). This proactive approach has included an explicit willingness to redesign traditional union policies and practices. In turn, this has led the union to develop an innovative approach to linking the contract and its negotiation and administration with the new paradigm rather than the limited approaches described earlier.

The significance of these aspects of the Shell Sarnia plant design, its setting and the extent of the ECWU's involvement, cannot be overstated. Change strategies in existing settings are shifting from a piecemeal focus on parts to a comprehensive focus on the whole organization (Trist 1983). As new computer-based manufacturing and information-processing technology becomes pervasive, office and manufacturing work will become more and more like continuous process work. Computer-directed or feedback-controlled systems give rise to integrated, flexible machine systems which resemble continuous process systems (Hirschhorn 1984; Susman 1986). Direct human intervention to control conversion uncertainties is minimal. Managing boundary transaction uncertainties emerges as the key focus of human activity (Pava 1981; Hirschhorn 1984). A recent OECD study (1986) found that new technology in the service sector 'shifts job scope and skills towards diagnosis, problem solving, the interface between systems, and, of course, customer contract' (38). In many situations realization of the full potential of this new technology will require work designed in the form of autonomous groups.

Furthermore, economic pressures favour the survival and growth of organizations which are both highly productive (in the broad sense of the term) and responsive to changing conditions. As many have argued (e.g., Reich 1983) it will be difficult if not politically impossible for North American industry to compete in international markets with a strategy that emphasizes low labour costs and high volumes of standardized products. To succeed, organizations must compete on high-value-added strategies and the capacity for flexible specialization (Piore and Sabel 1984) which entails the effective shifting of resources from one product/service niche to another. In this regard, the track record of organizations designed according to sts principles is superior to those which are not. A recent report in *Business Week* (29 September 1986) states that sts designed plants are '30% to 50% more productive than their conventional counterparts' and quotes a senior executive from Proctor and Gamble that his company's team-work plants were 'significantly more able (than their conventional counterparts) to adapt to the changing needs of the business.' Support for these performance claims can be found in the academic literature (e.g., Kochan, Katz, and McKersie 1986; Lawler 1978; Passmore, Francis, Haldeman, and Shani 1982). For example, regarding responsiveness, Kochan, Katz, and McKersie (1986) also point out that the new technologies make it 'technologically feasible to adapt production processes more readily to more specialized markets and shorten production runs, *provided that the system of work organization and human resource management is also flexible and adaptable*' (96; emphasis added). The authors then go on to list features of a typical sts plant which make possible this flexibility and adaptiveness. Such a comparative advantage should increase the rate of diffusion of the new paradigm.[1]

Finally, some recent union policies call for the integration of collective bargaining and new forms of work organization (e.g., Guillet 1984). Indeed, the proposed collective bargaining system for the new General Motors Saturn complex bears a strong resemblance to that of the Shell chemical plant. In sum, the ECWU local 800 is a 'leading part' (Emery and Trist 1973); it reveals a probable future in the present.

The data were collected by using three techniques: direct observation, interviews, and unobtrusive measures (Webb, Campbell, Schwartz, and Sechrest 1966). A fourth technique, questionnaires, was rejected because of the nature of my research question and the culture of unions in general and local 800 in particular. The case-study method assumes that patterns of causation are complex and difficult to discern. It demands data collection techniques which are highly flexible in order to allow exploration of emergent and unexpected directions. Questionnaires, however, deal with a relatively small set of variables and once pre-tested are difficult to alter. Furthermore, unions distrust 'experts armed with surveys instead of stop watches' (Strauss 1977). Finally, members of the local 800 are accustomed to dealing directly with issues. Questionnaires have only been used in a few very recent situations and they have all been developed by the members themselves (and management), not by external 'experts.'

Sources of data derived through direct observation include general membership meetings, informal meetings, a steward/members training school, and numerous presentations by the union (alone and with management) of their story to supportive and hostile audiences (management, union, and mixed). In addition, I attended, as a participant observer, a steward training school sponsored by a sister ECWU local from a traditional plant.

Respondents interviewed included current and past local union officials, rank-and-file members, ECWU officials beyond local 800, local and corporate level managers, and selected union officials from other unions. Interviews were semi-structured and were conducted in people's home, at the work site, in union offices, and in restaurants. Both individual and group interviews were conducted.

Sources of archive data obtained through unobtrusive measures include key public and internal documents. The former included the collective agreement, the plant philosophy statement, and the ECWU official policy on quality of working life. The latter included the manual of plant rules and procedures. (The collective agreement, table of contents of the manual of plant rules, and philosophy statement are reproduced in Appendices I, II, and III.) However, for reasons of confidentiality I was not permitted access to minutes of meetings of certain joint union management bodies (e.g., the union-management committee). Management, in particular, was concerned about references in the minutes to the behaviour of certain individuals. In order to compensate for this limit on my access to data sources, I conducted, at the suggestion and with the co-operation of both management and union, extensive interviews with the members of the relevant joint committees.

Data analysis and collection were intertwined, a continuous process of formulating concepts, identifying themes, and revising interpretations (Van Maanen 1979; Diesing 1971). The testing of provisional hypotheses involved the search for negative as well as confirming evidence. For example, early in my field-work I 'concluded' that the role of shop-steward, like its traditional counterpart, the first line supervisor, was redundant. However, by deliberately tracking the day-to-day activities of stewards I generated data which led me to discard this working hypothesis in favour of one in which the steward's role is more critical than ever. On a continuing basis, my observations and findings were checked out and subsequently verified or altered by respondents from the field site. This proved invaluable in helping me to refine my analysis. Finally, the dialectical nature of certain concepts was explored (Diesing 1971). For example, the overwhelming emphasis put on the 'mutuality of interest' and co-operation by both the work organization literature and the field site led me actively to search out evidence of conflicts of interest and competition. This search led me to some unexpected areas and, I believe, to some significant findings.

My findings are expressed in terms of tendencies among variables. This is because my research topic, like all social systems, tends to be very complex and unfinished and is characterized by events which are co-produced (Ackoff and Emery 1972). Essentially, my research develops grounded theory (Glaser and Strauss 1967) through what Kaplan (1964) has referred to as the 'pattern of model of explanation.'

The Research Site

Background and Setting

The Energy and Chemical Workers Union (ECWU) has a long history of innovation. In 1965, after a six-month strike, it negotiated one of the first Canadian collective agreements containing a major job security provision clause in the event of technological change. Partial job progression, the 35-hour week, and 12-hour shift schedules are other innovations successfully pioneered by the ECWU.

In addition to workplace changes, the ECWU has made significant changes in its internal structure and operation. In 1980–1, the

Canadian members of the Oil Chemical and Atomic Workers Union amicably parted ways with the international to form the independent ECWU. A major reason for this move was the desire by the Canadian members for more local decision-making power, which in this case meant not only nationally but at all levels of the union including regional councils and locals. The structure adopted at the ECWU founding convention puts strong emphasis on member, local, and regional participation and autonomy in the formulation and execution of union policy. Accordingly, the ECWU is one of the few industrial unions governed by a board of rank-and-file members, and not, as is common practice, by full-time elected officials. These internal changes strongly embody many aspects of the new paradigm of organization (e.g., equalizing of power among groups). It is not surprising, therefore, that the ECWU was one of the first North American unions actively to participate in a comprehensive program to develop a 'radically' different form of work organization.

In early 1977, at the invitation of Shell Canada, the ECWU agreed to participate in a joint union-management organization design task force. The task force was responsible for designing a new chemical plant in keeping with the principles of socio-technical systems thinking. The task force completed its work in late 1978. The chemical plant officially opened in November 1978 and began shipping product in early 1979. The story of this initial design phase is beyond the scope of this book. However, a detailed account of this critical phase has been written (Halpern 1983).

The chemical plant is located in Sarnia, Ontario, the heart of Canada's 'chemical valley.' Sarnia is a highly industrialized region with a population of 40,000. Approximately 50 per cent of the workforce is organized. The dominant union is the ECWU. The chemical plant is a world-scale facility with a 1986 replacement value of $300 million. The plant is a continuous operation, 24 hours a day, 365 days a year. It employs approximately 200 people, of which 138 are members of ECWU local 800.

Process or production operators average about 30 years of age and have a minimum of 12 years of education. The chemical plant produces polypropylene and isopropyl alcohol for domestic and international markets. Polypropylene, a plastic, is used in the manufacture of consumer items such as rope, carpets, mouldings, and automobile fixtures. Over twenty different grades are produced, each to high quality standards. Isopropyl alcohol is used in the manufacture of rubbing alcohol, solvents, and antifreeze. Polypropylene and isopropyl alcohol are 'performance' as opposed to 'specification' products. A specification product is one whose characteristics depend solely upon its physical and chemical specifications (e.g., density, boiling-point). According to Ondrack and Evans (1980) a performance product is one where 'outputs from the same batch will behave slightly differently for two different customers, depending on their own plant facilities and the products they are making (268). Accordingly, each product, like many services, has to be custom-made to meet the unique requirements of the client. The chemical plant's product market and innovative work organization is consistent with Piore's and Sabel's (1984) argument that economic growth will require organizations capable of 'flexible specialization.'

Organization Design

The Shell Sarnia chemical plant is designed according to the principles of socio-technical systems thinking. The fundamental importance and pervasive influence of the sts design principles are formally and explicitly acknowledged in a document titled *Plant Philosophy Statement*. This document was written in 1976 prior to the involvement of the ECWU. Its authors were the management members of the organization design task force. It was sanctioned by Shell senior management as the framework that would guide the design and ongoing operation of the chemical plant. It is still used as the major criterion for assessing redesign options. When the ECWU joined the design task force the philosophy statement existed only on paper; it had not yet been translated into concrete design features.

The philosophy statement is a lay person's version of the concepts and principles of socio-technical systems. For example, the term 'support system congruence' is not used but its meaning is clearly communicated in such sentences as, 'A system should be developed which permits any employee to undertake any task

TABLE 2
ORGANIZATION DESIGN OF THE SHELL SARNIA
CHEMICAL PLANT

TRADITIONAL DESIGN	ACTUAL DESIGN
1 person assigned to 1 task	team tasks
single-skilled workers	multi-skilled workers
7 departments	1 department
supervisors	co-ordinators
individual responsibilities	shared responsibilities
4 levels of management	3 levels of management
restricted information	shared information
discretion for some	discretion for many
status symbols	no artificial distinctions
hierarchy of classifications	one classification
pay for task performed	pay for knowledge
narrow participation, none in recruitment and selection	broad participation, including recruitment and selection
half time on days	two-thirds time on days
periodic, expert redesign	ongoing, participative redesign

required for the efficient operation of this plant ... The training and remuneration program must be designed accordingly.' Some design principles, however, are referred to directly (e.g., 'The social and technical systems are interrelated and must be jointly taken into account to achieve overall optimization'). Finally, explicit recognition is made of some of the values implicit in the socio-technical approach (e.g., 'error situation [sic] should be reviewed from a what we can learn standpoint and not from a punitive one').

What follows, in concrete terms, is a description of the plant design. To help clarify the innovative nature of the design, its features are compared to what would have emerged if the designers had followed the logic of scientific management, and indeed, the traditional design had been developed on paper by Shell management to satisfy internal budgetary requirements. The comparison between the two designs is summarized in table 2.

The complex and intricate relation between the sts principles and the plant design is best appreciated by viewing the plant as a system, not as a collection of parts. By 'a system,' I mean that each part has an effect on the performance of the whole plant and that no part has an independent effect on the whole plant (Ackoff 1973). For example, the dramatic increase in the amount of time an operator spends on days is a function of not only the innovative shift schedule but as well the way jobs are designed. While in a few instances there is a clear relation between a single sts design principle and the design feature (e.g., the principle of support-system congruence and the method of hiring), in most cases a feature incorporates several design principles. For example, the design of the software for the process computer system illustrates the principles of joint optimization, minimal critical specification and design, and human values. Furthermore, most of the principles are embodied in several design features. Taken as a system, the design of the chemical plant is a powerful example of one application of the design principles of socio-technical systems thinking.

The basic building block of the Shell chemical plant is the semi-autonomous work group or team. There are six process teams consisting of 18–20 members each and one 18-person craft team. In turn, each process team operates the entire plant including both the polypropylene and isopropyl alcohol lines. While the plant is made up of different operating areas and support functions, these are considered part of one department (i.e., the plant). Eventually all process team members will be able to operate most of the production process; to date the average team member can perform 70 per cent of the tasks required to operate the plant. In addition, each operator possesses a second skill in a support function (i.e., quality control, scheduling, warehouse, or maintenance). The craft team members are all journeymen tradesmen (i.e., electricians, pipefitters, millwrights, analysers, and instrument technicians). They are responsible for non-routine maintenance and for training those operators whose second skill is in a craft.

The building block of a traditionally designed plant would have been one-person-one-task units. The plant would be broken down into four operating and three support departments (i.e., scheduling, quality control, and maintenance). Process operators would be assigned full-time to operating activities (e.g., opening and closing valves) in one area (e.g., tank farm). All the support functions would be handled by full-time specialists.

Along with the team structure goes a redistribution of responsibilities in the innovative design. Teams are responsible for assigning work, technical training, authorizing overtime, and scheduling vacations. Traditionally, these functions would be handled by a first line supervisor. At Sarnia, the first line supervisor has been replaced by a co-ordinator. Freed of his/her former responsibilities the co-ordinator acts as a resource person and facilitator to the teams and represents the interest of management in relation to the teams.

The innovative organization design extends beyond the shop-floor into the management hierarchy. Traditionally, there would be four levels of management in each of the four operating and three support departments. At Sarnia there are three levels in the single department which is the plant. Furthermore, the usual practice of having separate managers for process operations and maintenance has been discontinued. The two positions have identical titles; operations managers and the incumbents are held jointly responsible for the overall effectiveness of the plant.

The plant's technical system is also significantly different from its traditional counterpart. The use of the process computer is the most dramatic example of this difference. Because of a limited knowledge of cause-effect relationships in the transformation process, software packages were designed to utilize the computer off-line. These programs allow the process operators to use the system as a resource for learning what combination of operational variables (e.g., temperature, pressure) is most effective. The computer answers queries put to it by operators regarding the effect of variables at different control levels but decisions are made by the operator. Furthermore, the information provided by the computer includes the economic implications of adjusting many of the operating variables (e.g., 'the incentive to attain target temperature of 225° is an improvement in yield out-turn to the extent of $550 per day') (Halpern 1983). Craft team members have corresponding degrees of operational responsibility and access to information. Traditionally, such high levels of operating discretion and access to technical and economic information reside exclusively with specialists in the engineering and planning functions.

Other differences between the chemical plant's technical system and a traditional plant concern the physical layout and the bagging operation. In order for the process teams to operate the entire plant effectively there is one instead of the two control centres envisaged by the design engineers (i.e., one for isopropyl alcohol and one for polypropylene). Since, in the new design, quality control has become an integral part of the process operator's role and is no longer a detached function performed by a specialist, the laboratory is more centrally located than is customary. Offices are laid out in order to enhance interaction, not to indicate status. Finally, the bagging operation is automated, eliminating a traditionally dull, mundane task.

Significant differences can also be seen in the design of the plant's support systems – in particular, classification and pay, hiring, and the work schedule. There is no hierarchy of job classifications. Process operators are paid on the basis of demonstrated knowledge and skills in both the process and second-skill areas. The more operators learn, the more they are paid. Team members play a central role in assessing peer competence. There is no limit on the number who can reach the top pay rate. Currently, 80 per cent of the process operators are at the top. For an entry-level operator the time normally required to reach this level is seven years. As a consequence of this innovative classification and pay system, local 800 has the highest median and average salary of any ECWU local.

In a traditionally design plant there would be a hierarchy of classifications, each limited to certain tasks, allocated a rate of pay, and assigned to specific individuals. Movement from one classification to another would occur only when a vacancy arose. Seniority would be the key consideration in filling the vacancy. As to hiring, teams interview and select new members from a short list provided by personnel. Also, teams play a large role in the selection of co-ordinators. When a vacancy occurs, both the teams and lower-level management separately rank-order their choices for replacement. The plant manager then makes the final decision. To date the candidate recommended by the teams has almost always been appointed. In a traditional plant all hiring and promotion would be handled entirely by management.

Finally, the work schedule is also significantly different than in a traditionally designed plant. Through a highly participative process, the workers and managers in the plant have designed an innovative work schedule, based on a mixture of 8- and 12-hour shifts, that minimizes shiftwork. In brief, teams rotate through a schedule that has four and one-half teams work 37 $\frac{1}{3}$ hours per week on a 12-hour rotating shift schedule covering the 24-hour-per-day process operation, and one and one-half teams, on average working 8-hour days in their second skill area (e.g., warehouse). This schedule allows process operators to spend two-thirds of their time on days (on 8- and 12-hour shifts) instead of one-half as in a traditional design. It also allows for more long weekends and a nine-day block of time off every nine weeks.

The organization design is not static. In keeping with the sts principle of incompletion it has undergone several revisions, both major and minor. For example, the classification and pay system has been completely overhauled. Other features which have been redesigned include quality control procedures, co-ordinator selection procedures, and the operation of the warehouse. All modifications have been consistent with sts design principles. Furthermore, both the ongoing monitoring and formal evaluation of the organization design are carried out by the employees themselves (management and union). Traditionally, the need for ongoing assessment would not be recognized, let alone involve workers. Periodic formal evaluations would be conducted exclusively by senior management and external consultants. At the chemical plant, 85 per cent of the plant population was actively involved in a six-month exhaustive evaluation that took place after the plant had been operating for five years.

Negotiations Theory

The process of gathering data, establishing categories, and developing the pattern underlying the Shell/ECWU collective bargaining system was an inductive one; the pattern is 'grounded' in the data. However, I did not enter the field site as a 'tabula rasa.' I was sensitized (Diesing 1971) to certain concepts and these no doubt guided my selection of data, choice of category, and ultimately my description of the pattern itself. In particular I drew upon two social science disciplines: negotiations theory (Bazerman and Lewicki 1985) and socio-technical systems thinking. The latter of course is the conceptual framework underlying the new paradigm of organization. It has been discussed in detail in chapter 1 and again in this chapter in the section dealing with the organization design of the Shell chemical plant.

The rationale for drawing upon negotiations theory has to do with the issue of conflict. No study of any workplace, and in particular a unionized workplace, would be complete without paying considerable attention to such a central phenomenon of life in organizations. In this regard the socio-technical system literature is weak. Not that conflict has been ignored in the sts tradition. Trist (1981) points out that a key feature of the new paradigm is a new negotiated order. And Pava (1980) compares the relative positions of competitive and collaborative values in the old and new paradigms. For the most part, advocates of the sts approach have devoted their energies to the conceptual and practical development of the collaborative values and strategies necessary for adaptation to turbulence. As a consequence, the issue of conflict is underdeveloped in the socio-technical literature. This underdevelopment is, in part, due to the fact that the most significant practical developments have been in the Scandinavian countries. In these countries, collaborative values are, relatively speaking, already well-established. Such is not the case in North America. Accordingly, for purposes of my study sts thinking has been linked up to negotiations theory and its focus, from a plurist perspective,[2] on conflict.

Negotiations theory assumes that there exist differences among actors (Kochan and Verma 1983) and that agreement is required in order to 'get things done' (Strauss 1978). Industrial relations theory has a long history of studying collective bargaining as formal negotiations (e.g., Perlman 1928; Commons 1934; Kerr and Fisher 1957; Kerr, Dunlop, Harbison, and Myers 1960; Barbash 1964). More recently, the notion that social orders (including collective bargaining) are always in some sense negotiated orders and that negotiations is an important substantive area of social science inquiry has been recognized (Zartman 1977; Strauss 1978; Bazerman and Lewicki 1985).

The negotiations literature suggests two areas in which to focus the analysis of my field: properties of negotiations, and the fit between types of conflict and conflict resolution strategies.

Concerning the first area, properties of negotiations, eight are relevant for my purposes. The first, the mixed-motive nature of the issues negotiated, means that the parties involved are separated by some conflicting interests and tied together by some common interests (Walton and McKersie 1965). Conflict, therefore, is accepted as a naturally occurring phenomenon that can have either positive or negative consequences for the different parties.

The second property, the complexity of the issues negotiated, refers to whether the content of the negotiations is routine or novel. Some negotiations about complex issues pertain to the ambiguity of legitimate boundaries, the third property of negotiations. Sometimes the boundaries of what can be legitimately negotiated are relatively unclear. When that is so, the outcome of negotiation is more precarious and often more complex (Strauss 1978). Complexity is also, in part, determined by whether negotiations are fundamentally about resources (e.g., dollars, goods, and services) or ideology (e.g., concepts, ideas, strategic approach.) (Eccles 1983).

The fourth property is the number of interests involved and their stake in the negotiations. Even the industrial relations literature which has traditionally stressed the dichotomy between labour and management has long recognized the existence of multiple interests within and across these two groups (Kochan and Verma 1983). This property suggests that the formation, duration, and dissolution of interests are important to understanding the negotiations process (Bacharach and Lawler 1981).

The fifth property is the type of power and its distribution between the parties involved in the negotiations. An extension of this property is that the more unequal the distribution of power the higher the likelihood that differences between parties will be suppressed, smoothed over, or ignored by the stronger party(ies), or not pursued by the weaker.

The sixth property is the temporal features of the negotiations – that is, their frequency and sequence. The seventh is the linkages among different sub-negotiation processes. Finally, the visibility of the negotiations to the various parties involved (i.e., their overt or covert character) is the eighth property.

The second area in which the negotiations literature suggests that I focus my analysis is the fit between types of conflict and conflict resolution strategies. The mixed-motive nature of issues and the range of objective and subjective differences in parties, goals, and perceptions suggest that the choice of conflict management strategy can be matched to the source of conflict. For example, Kochan and Jick (1978) found that the labour mediation process used in most public sector jurisdictions was ineffective in dealing with situations where the economic objectives of the parties were highly divergent but effective in handling situations where the parties needed to save face. The effective matching of source or type of conflict and resolution strategy is particularly significant because the lack of effective conflict management or resolution processes or procedures is likely to lead to lower levels of goal attainment for all parties (Kochan and Verma 1983).

My study of local 800 will draw upon the above two areas of negotiations theory in order to explore the relation between unions and new forms of work organization. However, my study will also contribute to the development of the negotiations discipline. As Bazerman and Lewicki (1985) point out in their recent review of the negotiations literature: 'Little empirical research has been done to create the basis for moving from theory construction to validation or drawing implications for action.' My study of the Shell/ECWU collective bargaining system is just the type of empirical research called for by Bazerman and Lewicki. It, therefore, contributes to the field by negotiations by helping to move it beyond 'broad and abstract conceptualizing about negotiating phenomena to more concrete analysis and practical application' (Kochan and Verma 1983).

4

The Chemical Plant Collective Bargaining System

The fundamental principles underlying collective bargaining (i.e., the structures and processes which encompass all the interactions between union and management) are highly developed, standardized, and deeply entrenched in the North American workplace. As I have argued in chapter 1, from the perspective of industrial unionism these principles or tenets are inextricably linked to scientific management. At the Shell chemical plant the outline of a new form of collective bargaining is emerging. This outline, while retaining some features of traditional collective bargaining, is a dramatic departure from the past. This emergent form represents a logical development of the new paradigm of organization and is based upon the design principles of socio-technical systems thinking.

This chapter is divided into three sections. The first describes the three separate but related components of the chemical plant collective bargaining system. The second section analyses the fit between the issues and structures and processes that make up these components and explains how the components function as a total system. The analysis includes a detailed discussion of the relation among alternative modes of regulating union-management relations, types of union-management conflict, and direct and indirect union member participation. Throughout the two sections the differences between the chemical plant collective bargaining system and the traditional system, as found for example in the nearby Shell refinery (also organized by the ECWU), are highlighted. These differences are summarized in table 3. The third section examines

TABLE 3
COMPARISON OF REFINERY AND CHEMICAL PLANT
BARGAINING SYSTEMS

REFINERY	CHEMICAL PLANT
1 major component (The collective agreement and its negotiation and administration	2 additional major components
Periodic negotiations	Continuous negotiation of many issues (e.g., grievance procedure, overtime equalization system)
Legal language	Everyday language
Low level of interest-group involvement	High level of interest-group involvement
Indirect member participation dominant	Direct member participation dominant
Regulation by rules	Regulation by rules and values

the relation between the design of the collective bargaining system and the design principles of socio-technical systems. It concludes with a discussion which speculates on the historical roots of the chemical plant's innovative bargaining system.

Components of the Collective Bargaining System

Collective bargaining at the chemical plant consists of three separate but related components: (1) the collective agreement and its negotiation and administration, (2) the *Good Works Practices Handbook* (GWPH) and its development and administration, and (3) the philosophy statement and its ongoing application and development. I will describe the three components in terms of two dimensions. These are the key characteristics of the issues with which they deal and of their structures and processes. The former consist of the basic type, inherent conflict, complexity, and stability of the issues. The latter consist of the degree of flexibility, type of control, dominant form of conflict resolution, form of union member involvement, extent of union interest-group involvement, and

TABLE 4
CHEMICAL PLANT COLLECTIVE BARGAINING SYSTEM

	THE COLLECTIVE AGREEMENT, CONTRACT NEGOTIATIONS, AND ADMINISTRATION	THE GWPH AND ITS DEVELOPMENT AND ADMINISTRATION	THE PHILOSOPHY STATEMENT AND ITS APPLICATION AND DEVELOPMENT
Characteristics of the issues			
Type	*Basic Issues Existential Type*	*Basic Issues Administrative Type*	*Adaptive*
Nature of union management conflict	Distributive	Integrative	Mixed
Complexity	Low	Medium	High
Stability	High	Medium	Low
Characteristics of the structures and processes			
Flexibility	Low	Medium	High
Control	Bilateral	Bilateral	Bilateral, unilateral
Dominant form of conflict resolution	Coercive	Expert	Moral, expert, formal
Dominant form of member participation	Indirect	Direct	Direct
Interest group involvement	Low	High	High
Dominant form of regulation	Fixed rules	Flexible rules	Values

mode of regulation of the structures and processes. These two sets of characteristics are crucial to understanding the complex pattern underlying the plant's unique form of collective bargaining. The description is summarized in table 4.

The Collective Agreement and the GWPH

The most startling and controversial feature of collective bargaining between local 800 and Shell is the length of the collective agreement. It is a mere 13 pages. By contrast, the agreement between sister ECWU local 848 and the adjacent Shell refinery is 73 pages long. The short agreement is a result of the distinction between what is considered part of the collective agreement and therefore handled in contract negotiations and administration, and what is considered part of the GWPH and therefore handled through a very different process.

For the most part, both the collective agreement and the GWPH deal with the same basic issues of wages and conditions of employment. These issues are: union recognition, union security, due process, job security, 'fair' pay, stable pay, a 'fair' work day and week, stable hours of work, extra pay for work beyond normal hours, extra pay for shift work, vacation entitlement, leaves of absences for personal reasons, union participation in health and safety, and employer funding of safety attire. It is Shell Canada policy not to bargain benefits (e.g., pensions, dental). All employees are covered by the same benefit package.

The collective agreement treats the above issues as an existential type or class of issues. By existential, I mean that the agreement recognizes the legitimacy of the issues and defines the extent of their existence. For example: 'Employees are entitled to three weeks vacation with pay at the completion of one full year's service.' By contrast, the GWPH treats these issues as an administrative type or class of issues. By administrative, I mean that the GWPH outlines in terms of guide-lines, rules, and procedures how the issues will be handled day-to-day. For example: 'Scheduling of vacations will be the responsibility of the teams. To assist the teams the following general guide-lines are provided.' Ten guides follow; for example,

'The splitting of one vacation week into units of one or more days for team members on a day schedule will be permitted, except during an "x" day week.'

In their existential form the issues embody the fundamental conflict of interest (Auberts 1963) between union and management. This conflict is distributive in nature. The issues are relatively simple and stable over time. In their administrative form the issues embody the conflict of rights (Auberts 1963) between union and management. This conflict is integrative in nature. The issues are moderately complex and somewhat unstable over time.

In the conflict of interests, the conflict is zero sum. A gain for the union is necessarily at the expense of management (and vice versa). Such is the nature of virtually all the conflict expressed by the issues contained in the collective agreement. For example, an increase in pay rate reduces profit. By contrast, in the conflict of rights, conflict is integrative or varying sum. Both sides can gain, or at least the gains of one side do not represent commensurate losses by the other. Such is the nature of virtually all the conflict expressed by the issues in the GWPH. For example, the administration of the progression system serves the interests of both union and management.

In their existential form the issues are simple in the sense that they are easily quantifiable (e.g., pay, seniority) and/or any cause-and-effect relation is straightforward (e.g., the relation between payment for call-out work and starting time) and they are routine (i.e., the same issues appear in each contract). However, in their administrative form the issues are moderately complex in the sense that while there are often several different and novel approaches to handling an issue (e.g., administration of the progression system), most issues are still quantifiable (e.g., definition of vacation week) and involve a straightforward relation between cause and effect: for example, the relation between procedures for overtime distribution and efficient coverage and fair distribution.

In their existential form the issues are relatively stable over time. With the exception of very unusual circumstances issues are not affected by changing conditions; however, the extent of their existence can and does change. By contrast, the administration of these issues is somewhat unstable over time. By definition, guide-lines, rules, and procedures are subject to changing and often unforeseen circumstances. For example, it was only through experience that union and management could test out, and subsequently revise, the progression system.

The Philosophy Statement

The third component of collective bargaining at the Shell chemical plant is the philosophy statement and its application and development. The philosophy statement deals with a large number of issues not covered in the collective agreement and the GWPH. These include the plant design (e.g., team responsibilities, role of the co-ordinator, grievances, the progression system) and other issues such as plant performance, the implementation of new technology, and product market conditions. However, the philosophy statement does not deal with such key business decisions as the choice of product market strategy and investment policies.

What is common to all these issues is that they are central to the plant's capacity to adapt to change. By adapt, I mean not just make minor modifications in either the plant or its environment but make changes in basic parameters.

Adaptive issues include both those which embody the conflict of rights and those which embody the conflict of interests between union and management. They display the corresponding distributive and integrative characteristics. Team complements is an example of the former. There is no overriding common basis for agreement; a gain for management (i.e., lower direct costs) is at the expense of the union (i.e., fewer members). The development of the teams in the direction of more autonomy is an example of the latter. The overriding common basis for agreement is the principles underlying the plant design; a gain for management (i.e., co-ordinators freed up to do long-range planning) co-exists with a gain for the union (i.e., higher-skilled members). However, some issues are mixed in nature. They embody both distributive and integrative conflicts.

Adaptive issues are complex and unstable over time. They are complex since many issues are novel (e.g., the introduction of new technology) and for many (e.g., the role of the co-ordinator) effective resolution involves dealing with several interacting variables. These issues do not comprise single factors acting through single chains of events, but rather are the product of a number of factors where doubt and uncertainty about what leads to what is the norm. Furthermore, they are complex because the essence of many issues (e.g., people's need for ongoing learning) cannot be quantified.

Adaptive issues are unstable in two ways. First, they are unstable in the sense that both the definition and the day-to-day application of many issues change over time and with experience. For example, many people are not consciously aware of their 'need' for ongoing learning until this need is activated (or reactivated) by some concrete experience. At any one time, therefore, the definition of what constitutes ongoing learning is temporary and its specific application is best seen as but one part of a never-ending developmental process. The second way that adaptive issues are unstable relates to the time between their recognition by union and management and the development of appropriate responses. Issues such as market conditions or technology are not inherently deterministic and mechanical. The complete consequences of such issues, including the nature, extent, and relative balance of conflict of rights and interests, are not only unpredictable, given sufficient time they are subject to influence by a wide range of factors including the actions of local union and management.

The issues handled in the collective bargaining system at the chemical plant display considerable variety in their characteristics. Not surprisingly, the structures and processes for handling these issues display a similar range of variety. The three structures and processes are the negotiation and administration of the collective agreement, the development and administration of the GWPH, and the philosophy statement and its ongoing development and application. Because, as explained earlier, the collective agreement and the GWPH deal with different forms of the same issues, I will deal with the first two structures and processes together, and then describe the third.

Contract Negotiation and Administration and the Development and Administration of the GWPH

The collective agreement is in effect for a specific period of time. Prior to its expiry, the local executive, who serve as the union negotiating committee, solicit proposals for changes from the membership. These proposals are then refined by the bargaining committee and presented as demands to management's negotiating committee. Negotiations ensue, the contract being negotiated as a total package. Initial proposals are often modified as negotiations progress. For example, during one round of negotiations one of the unions demands had been for total job security. However, the union settled for a clause protecting the membership from any job loss due to contracting out. Conflicts are resolved through the exercise of coercive economic power (French and Raven 1959). For example, in the initial round of negotiations between local 800 and Shell the wording of the due process clause was agreed upon only when the union had threatened to take a strike vote. Eventually, the two negotiating parties agree to a new contract. The union committee then puts the proposed contract to a vote of the general membership. A simple majority in favour of accepting the contract is required for it to be ratified. The agreement is then formally signed by the two negotiating parties and is legally binding on both parties for its term. Since the plant opened in 1978 there have been five rounds of contract negotiations resulting in two one-year and three two-year agreements. Once signed, the agreement requires virtually no administration – this is because the contract is written in terms of fixed specific rules which leave no doubt as to their application and are easily translated into behaviour (e.g., paycheques issued every two weeks).

Unlike the collective agreement, the GWPH does not have a fixed life, nor is it handled as a total package. The GWPH is continually negotiated (daily if necessary), or, more correctly, developed, and modified clause by clause. As several members, union officials, and managers put it, 'we negotiate 365 days a year.' Any manager, union official, member, or group of members can initiate the process of changing a clause in the GWPH. There are several starting points (e.g., the team, the steward, the local executive, the co-ordinator). The procedures for agreeing on changes vary considerably given the nature of the issue. For example, moving from an 8- to a 12-hour shift required the agreement of the union-management committee and a yes vote by 75 per cent of the membership. Changes in the system of overtime distribution were approved by the Union-Management Committee based upon the recommendation of a task force who consulted extensively with the membership. Adjusting the wording on gate passes was agreed to by the Team Norm Review Board acting alone. Conflicts over issues in the GWPH are resolved through a highly participative problem-solving process that attempts to satisfy the interests of all concerned. While the solution to some issues is relatively straightforward (e.g., parking), others (e.g., the progression system) require high levels of social and technical expertise. In sum, conflicts are resolved primarily through the use of expert power (French and Raven 1959), where the expertise is broadly distributed throughout the workforce (union and management).

Whether or not the GWPH is a legal contract binding on both parties has not been tested in the courts. It may belong to management exclusively under the principle of residual rights. It may be a joint document under the principle of shared rights. Or, because it is specifically referred to in the collective agreement, the GWPH from a legal perspective may be part of the collective agreement. Whatever its legal status, at the chemical plant the GWPH is viewed by both management and union as a binding, but flexible, joint agreement. All changes must be jointly agreed upon by both parties.

Because the clauses in the GWPH can be changed as the need arises, development and administration are best viewed as a continuous process. This was particularly true in the first two years of plant operation when the technology and the organization design were not yet 'settled.' During this period development and administration were handled by team members, teams, union officials, co-ordinators, and managers. Today, the plant has settled down. The GWPH, however, still requires some day-to-day administration. This is because it is written in terms of flexible rules, both general and specific. General rules (e.g., 'within reason an employee shall at his/her discretion order an overtime meal') involve some interpretation as to their application. Specific rules (e.g., 'all employees must wear a CSA approved safety hat'), like those in the collective agreement, leave no doubt as to their application and are easily translated into behaviour. Administration is handled almost exclusively by team members, teams, and co-ordinators. The extensive involvement, both during the initial developmental stage and since, of rank-and-file members in the administration of the GWPH is in part made possible because of the way it is written. It is not, as is often said in local 800, 'lawyer language.'

The structure and process for administering the GWPH are very similar to what Walton and McKersie (1965) call integrative bargaining, Herrick and Maccoby (1975) call mutual benefit bargaining, and Ronchi and Morgan (1981) call negotiation. For example, Walton and McKersie's list of tactics for maximizing the effectiveness of integrative bargaining includes:

– open-ended bargaining
– formulating agenda items as problems not solutions
– generation of several alternative solutions
– involving actors with a variety of perspectives
– involving actors with first-hand experience with the issues in question

The Development and Application of the Philosophy Statement

The third and final component of the collective bargaining system at the Sarnia chemical plant is the philosophy statement and its development and application. The adaptive issues with which it deals are handled through the team and joint union-management committee structure and process. The composition, mandate, and dominant decision-making style of the various elements of this component are described in chapter 5. The teams and committees are made up mostly of rank-and-file members, have broad mandates, and usually operate by consensus. The Union-Management Committee oversees the various permanent and ad hoc committees. The team and committee structure both continually negotiate or, more properly, develop and administer the adaptive issues. Issues are handled both separately and in clusters. In both cases, however, explicit attention is paid to the systemic relation between issues (e.g., team autonomy and the role of the co-ordinator). Adaptive issues, with the significant exception of the grievance procedure, legally 'belong' to management according to the principle of management rights. However, in practice most, but not all, of the issues are handled in a bilateral manner with enormous efforts made to ensure consensus between management and union.

The significance of the emphasis put on consensus and the unusual grievance process will be examined later in this chapter. Conflicts are resolved through moral, expert, and formal (i.e., management's) power.

The distinction between negotiate and develop and administer is more than just semantic. The common industrial relations use of the term 'negotiate' is much too narrow to capture the essence of the process. A distinguishing characteristic of the Shell/local 800 collective bargaining process is that in dealing with adaptive issues the participants work with an explicit set of values and an ideology. The specific values and ideology are incorporated in the plant philosophy statement. For the most part these values and ideology can be divided into three categories: assumptions and beliefs about people and their needs at work, normative statements about relations among individuals and groups, and the key concepts and most of the principles of socio-technical systems thinking. A partial list includes beliefs that 'employees are responsible and trustworthy; the social and technical systems are interrelated and must be jointly taken into account; groups of individuals can work together effectively as members of a team with minimal supervision; it is necessary to have a climate which encourages initiative, experimentation and generation of new ideas.' The salience of the philosophy statement in regulating adaptive issues cannot be overstated. The essence of the following statement taken from an interview with the first plant manager was echoed again and again by management and union members alike: 'The philosophy statement is the conscience for all design issues. For every major issue we come back to it, are we consistent or are we not.' Like rules, the above values regulate behaviour (e.g., a changed role for the co-ordinator). However, values cannot be 'administered' in the same way as rules. This point will be discussed more fully later in this chapter.

Fit between Issues and Structures and Processes

The Collective Agreement and Its Negotiation and Administration

In their existential form the basic issues of wages and working conditions involve distributive conflict and are relatively simple and stable in nature. The structure and process used to handle these issues are the collective agreement and contract negotiation and administration. This structure and process have little flexibility, is jointly controlled by union and management, uses coercive economic power as the dominant form of conflict resolution, involves predominantly indirect union member participation, involves little interest group participation, and uses fixed rules as the form of regulation.

Distributive conflict is appropriately handled by a structure and process that is relatively inflexible. Without their enshrinement in the collective agreement, issues like the very existence of the union, let alone members' rights concerning items like pay, would constantly be questioned. Periodic, rather than ongoing, negotiations provide the best balance between opportunities to break new ground and the need for protection and stability. Distributive conflict is necessarily resolved through coercive economic power. Since there is no common basis for agreement, there is not a real alternative to this form of conflict resolution.

Indirect, rather than direct, member participation is appropriate in dealing periodically with distributive conflict. During contract talks, immediate binding responses are required and the union must speak with one voice or risk being split by management, thereby weakening its bargaining position. This is not to say that the members do not participate directly. They do, but at an earlier stage, in the formulation of demands, and subsequently in the ratification of the agreement.

In their existential form basic issues are collective issues. The collective agreement is a contract between the union as a whole and management. The terms apply to everyone equally. It is therefore appropriate that the negotiation and administration of the agreement be carried out by representatives of the union as a whole. This is not to say that there is not any involvement of different interests inside the union. The union takes into account the power, needs, and objectives of its various interest groups when selecting which issues it will give priority to in any round of negotiations. However, the union negotiating committee speaks for the union as a whole and the membership as a whole ratifies the agreement.

Fixed rules are well suited to handling issues which involve distributive conflict and which are relatively simple and stable in nature. They clearly establish and limit the extent of any encroachments upon the rights of one or both of union and management. If agreements concerning distributive issues were not stated in terms of fixed rules but rather in terms of general values or even flexible rules they could be open to considerable interpretation. Given the relative imbalance of power between union and management, from the perspective of the former, interpretation could easily become abuse. Fixed rules (e.g., basic monthly salary for a journeyman is $2,430) prevent such abuse from occurring.

Fixed rules are also well suited to handling simple issues. They clarify and remove any possible confusion as to the fundamental meaning (e.g., 'for purposes of seniority the first day of operation shall be deemed March 1, 1978') of agreement about easily quantifiable issues. Flexible rules, of course, do the same. However, values with their general, open-ended nature would confuse, not clarify.

Fixed rules also regulate, in an appropriately mechanical manner, straightforward cause-and-effect relations. For example, 'Minimum payment for call-out work will be equivalent to four hours regular pay.' Again, flexible rules do the same. However, the organic nature of regulation inherent in values is inappropriate for such deterministic relations.

Finally, fixed rules are well suited to handling issues which are stable over time. The extra latitude made possible by values and ideals or even flexible rules is redundant.

The GWPH and Its Development and Administration

In their administrative form basic issues involve integrative conflict, and are moderately complex and somewhat unstable over time. The structure and process used to handle these issues is the GWPH and its development and administration. This structure and process is moderately flexible, is jointly controlled by union and management, uses expert power as the dominant form of conflict resolution, involves direct union member participation, involves considerable interest group participation, and uses flexible rules as the form of regulation.

Integrative conflict is appropriately handled by a structure and process which is somewhat flexible. On the one hand, a certain degree of flexibility is needed to assess the pros and cons of the numerous alternative means of putting into practice the day-to-day application of issues involved. As one union member put it, 'the GWPH allows us to change things as the need arises and change them again if they don't work out.' On the other hand, a certain degree of stability is required to codify the alternatives that do in fact work.

Integrative conflict is appropriately resolved through expert power. Expertise is required to assess the best alternatives for administering a principle. Coercive economic power is not necessary since agreement at the existential level provides a common goal.

Direct, rather than indirect, member participation is appropriate in dealing with day-to-day integrative conflict. Since immediate binding responses are not required, the expertise of all members, not just a representative few, can be tapped. This expertise is invaluable as the issues involved pertain directly to the day-to-day operation of the plant (e.g., overtime call-in procedures). The high level of direct participation does not mean that there is no indirect participation. The union executive, which is a representative group, has the final say concerning changes in the GWPH.

Given the common agreement reached between the union and management at the existential level, at the administrative level the union is able actively to involve its various interest groups. A powerful illustration of this involvement in local 800 concerns the revamping of the progression system. A special committee was struck to deal with this issue. On the union side, in addition to the appointment of the vice-president, an open election was held. The result was that a representative of a relevant interest group, workers with prior industry experience who are being used as trainers and therefore not progressing as quickly as the norm, was elected to the committee. 'I know it's heresy,' said one union official, 'but sometimes the interest of the local don't coincide with the interests of the members.'

Flexible rules are well suited to handling issues which involve integrative conflict and which are moderately complex and somewhat unstable over time. Since integrative conflict does not mean that a gain for one party is necessarily at the expense of the other, there is less need for the rigid protection of fixed rules. Furthermore, since many issues are easily quantifiable and/or involve a straightforward cause-and-effect relation, rules (fixed or flexible) as explained in the discussion about the collective agreement are better suited as the form of regulation than values. However, the fact that in their administrative form some issues can be handled in several ways and/or are somewhat unstable over time makes flexible rules, in sum, the best fit.

The Philosophy Statement and Its Development and Application

Adaptive issues involve both integrative and distributive conflict; they are complex and unstable over time. They are handled through a structure and process (i.e., the teams and joint committees) which are characterized by high flexibility; bilateral control; moral, expert, and formal power as the dominant forms of conflict resolution; direct union-member participation; high participation by union interest groups; and values as the mode of regulation.

It is interesting to note that Walton and McKersie (1965) observe that the most appropriate strategy for handling mixed issues (integrative bargaining to establish the maximum total sum, accompanied by hard distributive bargaining over shares) is very difficult to implement. Reasons for the difficulty include problems with separating the designation of shares from the search for additional gain, uncertainty concerning the bargaining orientation (distributive or integrative) at a given time of the other party, and the contradictory nature of the tactics required for integrative and distributive bargaining (e.g., 'what one has revealed in discussing the item in order to establish the greatest joint gain can weaken his position in bargaining over the shares of the gain').

However, unlike existential and administrative basic issues, the key characteristics of adaptive issues which explain their fit with their corresponding structure and process are not determined by their inherent conflict. Indeed, as I described earlier, in many cases the nature, extent, and relative balance of types of conflict are unpredictable and subject to influence. Instead, the key factors are the high levels of complexity and instability which can only be addressed by the problem-solving approach characteristic of integrative bargaining supplemented by explicit reference to values. The bargaining approach (i.e., contract negotiations) characteristic of distributive issues is not required. Walton and McKersie's pessimistic scenario for the handling of mixed issues is thereby avoided.

As pointed out earlier, it is important to bear in mind that some critical complex issues (e.g., investment strategies) are not handled in the collective bargaining system. No doubt aspects of these issues could 'fit' within the contract. Indeed, some aspects of some of the issues (e.g., team size) currently handled in this component of the bargaining system are easily quantifiable. With a different balance of power between the two parties, these aspects would probably be handled through the collective agreement. However, this does not undermine the relevance of the classification system presented here. Complex, qualitative issues cannot be handled *entirely* through a rigid rule-based structure and process. Unions, in particular, have great difficulty in dealing with such qualitative issues. As Sandberg (1986) points out, this is due in large part to the fact that unions are used to dealing with issues (e.g., wages, hours of work) which are characterized by relatively well-developed union objectives, clearly formulated demands (often quantified), demands based on workers' own practical experience, and clearly delimited, short negotiation situations.

Complex and unstable issues are appropriately handled by a structure and process which is highly flexible. If not, issues would be prematurely defined or treated as resolved when they can change dramatically over time. For example, the introduction of $1.2 million of new technology into the warehouse was initially expected to include a certain type of computerized information system and adversely to affect the process operator progression system. If union and management had dealt with these effects by negotiating the usual clauses in a traditional collective agreement (e.g., advance notice of lay-offs) certain actions would not have been explored. In this case, union and management chose to establish an ad hoc task force which selected a different computer system and 'designed out' the adverse affects of the new technology on the progression system.

Flexibility is also required in order that novel configurations of people and approaches can be used to handle novel issues, and, under conditions of novelty, experience is no longer the best or even a good teacher (Ackoff 1973). For example, the formal evaluation of the performance of the plant design was a unique experience for union and management. Even visits to other organizations proved of little value in helping them come to grips with the issue. Union and management, therefore, designed their own strategy. This strategy included setting up ad hoc task forces, involving personnel external to the plant who normally had few interactions with it, and developing tailor-made methods and techniques for gathering different types of data. Flexibility, therefore, allows union and management to deal with novelty by experimentation.

Differences over the definition and resolution of complex and unstable issues are best handled through a combination of moral and expert power. Obviously considerable expertise is required. The need for moral power, while perhaps not so obvious, is just as important. Moral power is needed in two ways. First, the ability to interpret and apply values is a kind of expertise; they provide direction when technical expertise (i.e., cause-effect relations) cannot. This point is developed later in this section. Second, moral power is required since a shared set of values is necessary for effective performance of organization when faced with a complex and unstable environment (Emery and Trist 1973). The scope of the evaluation issue, for example, was broadened to include items of concern only to the union (e.g., attendance at union meetings, time spent on union business in team meetings). The grounds for broadening the scope were moral ones, appeals to fairness and the sts design principle of joint optimization.

In addition to expert and moral power I found occasional, but significant, examples of formal power. For example, the decision to add a second co-ordinator to each team was made unilaterally by management. These exceptions are possible because of legal distribution of powers between management and union. However, within the boundaries of the issues considered, they are exceptions. Both sides go to great lengths to ensure that decisions are reached by consensus. For example, the laboratory has been redesigned several times in an attempt to satisfy all concerned. Even in the case of the second co-ordinator, joint union management task forces were established to clarify the roles of the two co-ordinators and develop a plan, since implemented, for a return to just one. By management not exercising its formal powers, both management and union are likely to develop the shared values so crucial to handling adaptive issues. This is consistent with Emery's (1976) proposition that the functional demands on modern organizations (i.e., to reduce turbulence) will lead to the democratization of work. This is not to imply that legislative change is not a necessary step in the **process** of democratizing work. This author would agree with Schneider (1985), who argues that 'It is precisely the interplay of strong formal rights and robust informal practice that makes for effective worker participation'(24).

Direct, rather than indirect, member participation is appropriate for dealing with complex and unstable issues. The more expertise that can be drawn upon, the greater the likelihood of resolving the issue. Furthermore, the emphasis on direct participation allows a matching of people with relevant expertise with particular issues. For example, one of the process operators on the task force dealing with the introduction of new technology into the warehouse was chosen because of his competence in understanding computer systems. Direct participation is also appropriate as it allows values to have shared meanings and emotional valence for people. Lengthy discussions, both formal and informal, take place as to the meaning of such sentences in the philosophy statement as 'employees are responsible and trustworthy.' Direct participation is in part made feasible by the lead time involved in dealing with adaptive issues. Some of the issues handled in the GWPH have a 24-hour time frame; those in the collective agreement usually involve a one- or two-year time frame. By contrast, adaptive issues usually have at least a two-year horizon.

Given the complex and unstable nature of adaptive issues, high levels of interest group involvement are effective in ensuring that an issue is looked at from various perspectives. Effective handling of an adaptive issue requires that resolution is appropriate not to just one part of the organization but to all parts. A good example of this involvement is the union membership on the committee charged with revamping the progression system. As explained earlier, a vote was held which resulted in the election of a representative of relevant interest group, workers with prior industry experience who were suffering under the terms of the system in place. However, the effective resolution of adaptive issues requires that responses fit the membership as a whole, not just the sum of its interest groups. In the example cited, the vice-president of the union was also a member of the committee.

Finally, and perhaps most important, values are well suited to regulating complex and unstable issues. The strengths of the value-based approach to regulation can be best seen by contrasting them with the weaknesses of the rule-based approach. This contrast applies the ideas of Gustavsen and Hunnius (1981), who critiqued the rule-based approach to regulation in the context of health and safety.

The general thesis underlying the rule-based approach to collective bargaining, both in general and in the example of the chemical plant, is that agreements are encroachments upon the basic freedom of one or both of the parties. In order both clearly to establish and to limit the extent of any encroachment it is in the interest of the two parties to state any agreement in terms of clear, precise rules. Rules in turn lead to administrative practices (e.g., traditional contract administration) and roles (e.g., traditional shop-stewards) based on subsumption decisions. A subsumption decision requires the matching of facts to rules. The solution to a problem is defined by finding the right rule or rules to fit a set of given facts. This is the type of decision made by the courts.

The general thesis underlying the value-based approach to regulating adaptive issues developed at the chemical plant, including the handling of conflict, is that effective regulation is not possible through the use of rules. Rules, as I argued earlier, impede progress. It is therefore in the interest of union and management to state agreements concerning adaptive issues in terms of values. These provide direction where there is doubt as to causal links. Values in turn lead to administrative practices (e.g., working-through and roles (e.g., local 800's shop-stewards) based on means-end decisions. A means-end decision is a fairly open selection of means guided by the ends one wants to achieve. The concept of working-through and the role of the shop-steward will be discussed in chapter 5.

Notwithstanding the advantages described earlier, the rule-based approach has five important disadvantages. The first, an inability to deal with complex issues, has already been discussed. The second is that change is generally not treated as part of a long-term holistic developmental process, but instead as a short-term adaptation of a given rule. Hence, adaptive issues which demand a developmental perspective are ignored or short-changed. This disadvantage is exacerbated when the rules are contained in a collective agreement and are effectively frozen between rounds of contract negotiations. The problems with this one-step-at-a-time approach to progress was evident in the heyday of scientific management: 'the working rules of trade unions are built up gradually one or two at a time. This leads to an atomistic consideration of their effects, which may cause their effects as a whole to be overlooked ... Each of the individual rules may seem quite fair and defensible, and yet as a body they may produce an effect which no one intended and which is inimical to the interests of the workers themselves' (Slichter 1941, 578). The third and fourth disadvantages of the rule-based approach are of particular significance to unions. They are issues of burden of proof and measurement. Traditionally, in order for a union to respond to a member's problem (i.e., file a grievance) during the life of a collective agreement, a rule must be violated. Activities and processes are determined unilaterally by management unless there are rules prohibiting them. It is up to the union to show cause that a rule has been violated. When the use of rules is a bad fit with the nature of the issue, proof of violation is virtually impossible.

Finally, the rule-based approach turns the resolution of problems, to a large extent, into problems of measurement and interpretation of measurement. Problems, therefore, require experts both local (e.g., shop-stewards and industrial relations specialists as lawyers) and external (e.g., regional representatives, staff specialists). As a consequence the possibilities for active involvement on the part of the members who experience the problem are severely limited. They usually have to stand back and await the judgment of the experts, if and when they are available. Furthermore, given the relative resources of management and union, the former's experts usually outnumber those of the latter.

At the chemical plant, the regulation of the development and application of the philosophy statement is based on values. The relative advantages of this approach to regulation counter the disadvantages of the rule-based approach. Unlike rules, values allow union and management to deal effectively with complex issues. They provide direction in situations where end-states, starting points, and means cannot be precisely described in advance (e.g., developing semi-autonomous teams). In addition, since values are not absolutes but are subject to constant reformulation as knowledge and understanding of people and their environment expands (Ackoff 1973) they are well suited to dealing with the unstable nature of complex issues. At the chemical plant, union and management, on a regular basis, ask their members/employees for behavioural examples of the values contained in the philosophy statement. In this way the concrete public meaning of, for example, 'employees are trustworthy and responsible' develops over time.

In a similar vein Emery and Trist (1973) stress the need for changing values as a basis for purposeful adaptation to turbulence. Values, both individual and communal, are the basis of all regulative processes and underlie all strategic and tactical responses. They

have overriding significance for members of the field. Values have always arisen as the human response to persisting areas of relevant uncertainty ... Typically, these are not just goals or even the more important goals. They are ideals like health and happiness that, at best, one can approach stochastically. Less obvious values, but essentially of the same nature, are the axioms and symbols that lead us to be especially responsive to certain kinds of potentialities ... It is essential to bear in mind that values are neither strategies nor tactics and cannot be reduced to them ... For large classes of events their relevance no longer has to be sought in an intricate mesh of diverging casual stands but is given directly and in almost binary form by references to the ethical code. (Emery and Trist 1973, 88–9)

Similar arguments are put forward by the ethnomethodologist Cicourel (1973) and various writers in the information-processing branch of organization theory. Cicourel uses the terms 'interpretive procedures' or 'deep structure' for values, and argues that they are necessary for any collaborative approach to regulation.

Interpretive procedures as opposed to 'surface' rules (norms) ... are constitutive of the members' sense of social structure organization. The acquisition of interpretive procedures provides the actor with a basis for assigning meaning to his environment or a sense of social structure; thus orienting him to the relevance of 'surface' rules or norms. Plus ... the interpretive procedures provide a sense of social order that is fundamental for normative order (consensus or shared agreement) to exist or be negotiated or constructed ... the learning and use of general rules or norms and their long-term storage, always require interpretive procedures for recognizing the relevance of actual changing scenes orienting the actor to possible courses of action, the organization of behavioural displays and their reflective evaluation by the actor. (31–2)

From an information-processing perspective, Galbraith (1973, 1977) points out that when uncertainty and information-processing requirements are low, means-ends relationships are likely to be relatively predictable. Control or regulation, therefore, can be achieved by the specification of various standards, rules, and procedures. However, when information-processing requirements are high and means-end relationships are uncertain, control or regulation is characterized by the monitoring and evaluation of output (Ouchi 1977), by the specification of general goals (but not the means), and by establishment of sets of norms and expectations regarding appropriate behaviours (Van de Ven and Morgan 1980).

In addition to regulating complex issues values allow union and management to have an interactivist (Ackoff 1973) perspective on planning. Interactivists are dissatisfied with both the current state of affairs and the way they are going. Pursuing ideals helps them to try to do better than the best that appears to be possible now. Interactivists try to change the nature of systems so they can prevent, not merely prepare for, problems and create, not merely exploit, opportunities. This introduction of new technology into the warehouse is a good example of the former. The development of a flexible grievance process (see below) is an example of the latter. It, in part, created some of the necessary conditions for union and management to redesign their progression system. Finally, values also effectively deal with the other disadvantages of a rule-based approach. They treat change not as a short program, but according to the GWPH as an 'evolutionary process of continuous examination, evaluation and redesign.'

Another disadvantage of the rule-based approach to regulation, the requirement of burden of proof, is according to the GWPH replaced by 'continuous examination by employees to assess to what extent objectives were being met, whether past objectives, administrative procedures, roles, policies, etc. were still desirable or realistic and to generate appropriate revisions/changes.' Finally, the excessive reliance on experts because of the rule-based emphasis on measurement is countered in the value-based approach by an emphasis on democratic participation and control. Its premise is that the main responsibility for handling most issues in the plant should be with the workers. It aims to develop and distribute expertise among the workers themselves and to emphasize the type of expertise developed by working in the chemical plant. The approach to health and safety is an example of this new direction. Both the company and union health and safety specialists are used as resources, not experts. It is the members who are most active in shaping and carrying out the health and safety program.

The grievance process is a particularly informative example of the fit between the issues and the characteristics of the structure and process of this third component of the collective bargaining process. Local 800 has come under severe criticism from other unions for not including its grievance process in the collective agreement. Typically, a contract would specify the definition of a grievance, the levels in the grievance process, for each level the time period in which the grievor must receive a response to his/her grievance, and the grievor's right to be represented by a union official. Local 800 and Shell management have replaced this rather inflexible, rule-based, representative approach with one which is flexible, value-based, and directly involves the members.

A grievance is defined, according to the GWPH, as 'any problem.' The grievance process consists of four levels: the team, the Team Norm Review Board, the plant manager, and an external arbitrator. No time limit is associated with any level. At first, the team as a whole with the co-ordinator tries to resolve the issue. If the issue involves disciplinary action the team may make a recommendation to the co-ordinator. Usually, teams choose not to take any formal role in a discipline case. The steward is usually involved but not as a spokesperson for the grievor. If the team and the co-ordinator are unable to resolve the issue or if it clearly is a plant-wide issue, it goes to the TNRB. On more than one occasion the TNRB has refused an issue stating that the team had not sufficiently pursued its resolution. The TNRB operates by consensus with any one person having the right to veto a decision. In cases of discipline the TNRB makes a recommendation to the plant manager. In handling issues the TNRB has the advantage of several different perspectives; the grievor, the seven teams; the co-ordinators, the union executive and plant management. If necessary additional resources are called upon. The formation of special fact-finding and problem-solving task forces is quite common. The grievor normally acts as his/her own spokesman. If the TNRB cannot resolve a disciplinary issue it goes to the plant manager, who makes a unilateral decision which the union may take to arbitration. At all levels (except the arbitrator who has yet to be involved) the philosophy statement plays the key (but not only) role in determining appropriate action. As of January 1985, eleven formal grievances had been processed, none in the last two years. Eight of the eleven had to do with discipline, complex issues where the nature of the transgression had to be clarified, the significance of any extenuating circumstances weighed, and the appropriate penalty determined. Only three of these reached the TNRB; none reached the plant manager. The people directly involved, therefore, resolved the grievances.

The reason for the union's support for such a non-traditional process is, according to the national representative, its effectiveness. 'The proof of the pudding is in the eating. It is the best system for resolving problems that I've seen in any plant.' The local executive and members share this view, stating that issues are typically 'resolved thoroughly and fairly, though sometimes slowly.'

Despite its effectiveness the above grievance process was temporarily abandoned when a particular novel, complex, and significant issue arose, the redesign of the process operator progression system. Its temporary replacement is a further example of the nature of the fit between the characteristics of the issues and the structure and process of developing and applying the philosophy statement.

The new progression system affected everyone's immediate and long-term income and sense of equity. Union and management, therefore, were very concerned that any grievances be quickly and fairly resolved. A two-level process was established. The first consisted of a four-person committee with two management and two union representatives. The latter include the vice-president and a rank-and-file member, both of whom have widespread reputations for fairness. The committee operated on a consensus basis. If they were unable to reach a decision or if the 'grievor' disagreed with their consensus the issues was referred to the plant manager. Eleven people approached the committee with complaints about the new progression system. None reached the plant manager.

A complementary perspective on this aspect of the bargaining system, the fit between values and novel issues, is provided by a philosopher, Shwayder (1965). He distinguishes two types of rules: those which operate to modify independently existing forms of behaviour and activity and those which create new forms of behaviour and activity. The first are called restrictions and the second enabling rules. The fixed and flexible rules that regulate the collective agreement and the GWPH are examples of the former – they are prescriptive injunctions. The ideals and values that regulate the third component of the collective bargaining process are examples of the latter. According to Shwayder such 'rules' 'open up entirely new locales of action and activity to those capable of mastering them. They enable us to act in new ways otherwise beyond our power. To enhance our potentialities by cutting new tools for new jobs which we could otherwise not undertake or even so much as hope to undertake ... Conformity to enabling rules in the first place one attains a somewhat higher level of behaviour than he previously occupied.'

The Collective Bargaining System as a System

The previous section is a partial description of how the collective bargaining system functions as a system. Discussed were the relation between the first two components of the system (the agreement and its negotiation and administration and the GWPH and its development and administration) and how the overall matching of issues and structures and processes allows the particular advantages of each component to be fully exploited while avoiding the disadvantages. The chemical plant bargaining system, therefore, overcomes the inherent 'antithetical relationship' (Walton and McKersie 1965) involved in the simultaneous handling of distributive and integrative issues.

However, to complete my description of the collective bargaining process as a system it is necessary to examine the relations between its third component (the philosophy statement and its development and application) and the two others, and to articulate the dominant characteristics of the overall system. Concerning the first, two points are relevant. First, some of the outcomes of deliberations in the third component sometimes result in a change in items in both the collective agreement and the GWPH. For example, the major redesigns of both the process operator and craft progression systems were handled by the teams and selected committees using the philosophy statement as a guide. The new design resulted in changes in both the contract and the GWPH. Rates of pay, a distributive issue, were appropriately altered in the agreement while progression procedures (e.g., testing), an integrative issue, were appropriately altered in the GWPH. One highly complex issue, the role of the co-ordinator, is also included in the GWPH. It is an exception though, and reflects the fact that the three components are, to a small extent, ideal types.

The second way the three components are linked is less obvious but much more significant. It involves the use of contentious behaviour (Pruitt 1983), usually associated with distributive bargaining. Contentious behaviour consists of all those actions that are designed to elicit concessions from the other party. These include threats and coercion. According to Pruitt, contentious behaviour has traditionally been assumed to militate against the development of integrative agreements (Walton and McKersie 1965; Deutsch 1973; Blake and Mouton 1979), and he cites research evidence supporting this assumption (Pruitt and Carnevale 1982). Pruitt (p 47) identifies four reasons why this should be true:

1 Contentious behaviour ordinarily involves standing firm on a particular proposal that one seeks to foist on the other party. This is incompatible

with the flexibility about means that is an important element of successful problem-solving.

2 Contentious behaviour encourages hostility toward the other party by
a principle of psychological consistency. This diminishes one's willingness to contribute to the other's welfare and hence one's willingness to
devise or accept jointly beneficial alternatives.

3 Contentious behaviour encourages the other party to feel hostile and
engage in contentious behaviour in return. A conflict spiral may ensue
in which both parties become increasingly rigid and progressively more
reluctant to take actions that benefit the other.

4 Contentious behaviour signals to the other party that one has a win/
lose orientation, calling into question the possibility of achieving a
jointly beneficial agreement. In other words, it tends to reduce the
integrative potential perceived by the other party.

These reasons underlie a common argument against the long-term
feasibility of new forms of work organization: namely, that you
cannot wear two hats at the same time. However, they run counter
to the experience at the chemical plant which has maintained
its system while negotiating five contracts in both good and bad
economic times. Resolution of this inconsistency is found in Pruitt
and Gleason's (1978) work on contentious behaviour and problem-
solving. They conclude that under some circumstances the former
can make the latter more likely or contribute to its effectiveness.
This can occur in two ways: by encouraging the other party to face
the controversy when he/she benefits from the status quo, and by
underlining one's areas of firmness (thereby identifying for both
parties the arena for problem-solving). The advantages of this
behaviour can, of course, be easily offset by its obvious pitfalls (e.g.,
initiating a conflict spiral). Pruitt (1983) suggests some ways to
avoid such consequences. These include using contentious tactics
to defend basic interests rather than to provide a particular solution
to the controversy, and employing deterrent rather than compellent
threats. This particular perspective on contentious tactics is sub-
stantiated by two significant developments in the chemical plant.
In turn, this perspective explains a critical link between the three
components of the collective bargaining system.

The first development involved the right to due process and the accompanying grievance procedure. The first collective agreement was silent on both issues. Prior to start-up, the two parties had agreed that at some point an appropriate system would be designed. However, this understanding on the union side involved essentially only the national office; rank-and-file members had not yet been hired. In fact the first agreement was negotiated by the national representative and 'ratified' by the one and only local member who had joined by that time. During the first year of operation several members felt that management had acted unilaterally and unfairly concerning the amount of time operators spend developing their second skill. As a result, a key union demand at the second round of negotiations was that the right to due process be included in the collective agreement. Management refused. The union then underlined its area of firmness by taking a strike vote (100 per cent in favour of the executive). Management gave in the day before the union was in a legal strike position. However, the union used contentious tactics only to defend a basic interest. At no time did they insist on a specific grievance process. In fact, the grievance process was designed through the third component in the collective bargaining system and then included in the GWPH. Subsequently the grievance process has twice been altered to reflect learning from practice.

The second development involved the redesign of the craft team progression system which occurred in late 1984 and early 1985. For quite a while the members of the craft team had been concerned that they were not duly recognized for their role in the chemical plant. In addition to regular maintenance duties they also trained process operators in their second skill – a role unique in the industry. Management, while acknowledging the issue, did not feel it warranted immediate attention. While they had some concerns about the maintenance function, they were basically satisfied (for the short term) with the status quo. The union was successful in 'encouraging' management to confront the issue by employing contentious tactics. Craft team members refused overtime call-ins. Process operators temporarily 'forgot' some of their higher-level craft skills. The union put forward a contract demand that craft team members be guaranteed a meal every time they were called in off-shift. Management finally agreed to form a joint task force to address the craft team concerns. At no time did the union present or judge any solution to the issue beyond indicating that the current situation favoured by management was not acceptable. Once their task force was formed, all contentious behaviour ceased. Even the bargaining demand, which was a ploy to get the task force formed, not a serious solution, was dropped. Consistent with the style of the third component of the collective bargaining system the task force was made up of different stakeholders (e.g., representatives from all trades, the union executive, process operators, management, and co-ordinators). The task force approached the issue from a systems perspective (e.g., the nature and function of plant maintenance, skill levels, procedures, training, pay, supervision). Three months later the maintenance system had been significantly redesigned.

The above examples are also very significant as they are strong evidence of a very fundamental change in the overall nature or system characteristics of collective bargaining as practised at the chemical plant. Walton and McKersie in their 1965 landmark study of labour negotiations observe that 'negotiations cannot be divided into phases and a bargainer cannot readily shift from an integrative to a hard distributive orientation. Rather, it is easier for him to maintain a more or less consistent orientation throughout negotiations, which from the veiwpoint of achieving a minimum level of satisfaction, may be the distributive orientation'(167). In the chemical plant the separation of the contract and the GWPH does, to a certain extent, divide up negotiations into discrete phases. However, there is still a 'consistent orientation' but it is a collaborative one rather than a competitive or distributive one. Time and time again union and management stated the desire to limit contract negotiations strictly to wages. The strongly shared preference is to handle all items through the second and third components. However, in the two examples just cited union and management 'negotiated' wage rates (including increases) through the philosophy statement and the team and joint committee structure and process. The chemical plant collective bargaining process may suggest a basic shift in its overriding governing value (Pava 1980). Such a shift is predicted by Trist (1983), who argues: 'it is not entirely fanciful to think that even in North America, collaboration might become primary in labour-management relations, while competition would be reserved for more familiar contract issues. In a turbulent environment the finding of common ground provides the basis of survival for both management and labour and thence of wider society' (46). This shift in the relative balance between competition and collaboration is an example of the shift in the underlying pattern of social values and relations.[1] According to Pava (1980), in the old paradigm the overriding governing value is competition; fractional warfare of varying degrees limits and constrains collaborative relations. Collaboration is required but is only a subordinate value. In the emerging paradigm collaboration becomes the governing value, which limits and constrains fractional competition. Competition is still required, but it now expresses the subordinate value.

The Design of the Collective Bargaining System

The fundamental nature of the chemical plant collective bargaining system and the design principles of socio-technical systems thinkings are inextricably linked. First, the bargaining system incorporates several design principles. Second, it enhances the development of some of the work organization applications of the principles. Finally, the effective functioning of the collective bargaining system is dependent upon the perspective, skills, and norms developed in local 800 members by the organization design.

Design Criteria

The nature of the bargaining system is a logical outcome of the application of the sts design principles of support-system congruence, minimal critical specification, and variance control. The principle of support-system congruence states that organization support systems should be designed to reinforce the behaviours, values, and attitudes which the overall organization is designed to elicit. In the chemical plant, the foreword to the GWPH makes just this point with regard to collective bargaining. The foreword highlights certain aspects of the plant philosophy (i.e., free-flowing communication and direct individual and team participation) and goes on to state that the collective agreement is 'consistent with this philosophy.' The foreword also specifies that the contract and the GWPH are designed to reinforce the development of two major overall design objectives.

Flexibility based on trust can, in this organization, replace the traditional relationship founded on inflexible strict legal interpretation of carefully documented contractual relations. ... One of the key premises of our organization design is that the Chemical Plant is a 'learning organization.' In other words, in our organization, there is a continuous examination by employees to assess to what extent objectives were being met, whether past objectives, administrative procedures, roles, policies, etc. were still desirable or realistic and to generate appropriate revisions/changes. This *Good Work Practices Guidebook* is, therefore, also intended to permit the evolutionary process of continuous examination, evaluation and redesign by employees without the traditional constraints imposes by a Collective Agreement.

The principle of minimal critical specification states that no more should be specified than is absolutely essential. The spirit and letter of this principle is reflected in the foreword to the collective agreement: 'The purpose of the agreement which follows is to establish an enabling framework' and the foreword to the GWPH: 'the agreement developed between your management and ECWU local 800 contains only those items that were felt to be essential.' It is interesting to note that in the initial negotiations over what was 'absolutely essential' and therefore to be included in the collective agreement the union won the right to the automatic deduction of union dues for all employees covered by the contract. Local 800 is the only local in all of Shell Canada's unionized facilities to have negotiated such a clause. Specifying minimal critical parameters is of course crucial to developing an organization's capacity to learn and adapt. If more is specified than is needed, options are closed that could be kept open (Cherns 1976). The collective agreement provides the security and stability upon which the flexibility of the remaining two components of the collective bargaining system is based.

The principle of variance control states that the information, skills, and authority needed to control things that could go wrong (i.e., variances) in the technical subsystem should be located where the variance is likely to occur. In the chemical plant, union and management have extended the definition of variance to include the administration of the GWPH and the team and committee structure. For example, the foreword to the GWPH states: 'In the development of the quasi-autonomous work teams at the Chemical Plant, information on company policies and administrative practices required by the employees in the decision-making process are provided in the *Good Work Practices Guidebook*.' Problems with the administration of the GWPH and the development of the team and joint committee structures are likely to occur first in the day-to-day operation of the plant. Consistent with the principle of variance control local 800 has, therefore, delegated to rank-and-file members many of the responsibilities typically reserved for union officials. (A detailed description of the allocation of responsibilities inside the union follows in chapter 5.)

The Shell/local 800 approach to collective bargaining is a dramatic departure from tradition. As I explained in chapter 2, in many quality-of-working-life projects, contract negotiations and administration, *the* central organization support system, are handled in a manner which usually contradicts, not reinforces, the goals of these projects. Furthermore, in both traditional and 'QWL' organizations the contract is designed according to the principle of total specification and handled predominantly by representatives. Union and management are well aware of the significance of their approach, accurately describing their collective agreement in the foreword of the GWPH as 'historic.' Indeed, Davis and Sullivan (1980) equate the significance of the chemical plant collective agreement for the evolving post-industrial era with the engineering design in Volvo's auto assembly plant at Kalmar, Sweden (Augren, Hansson, and Karlsson 1976; Augren et al 1984). At this plant, for the first time in the history of auto assembly, both the classical machine-paced moving assembly line technology and the one-person–one-task building block of scientific management were rejected in favour of flexible assembly 'chariots' and a limited form of semi-autonomous work group.[2]

Enhancement of STS Design Principles

In addition to incorporating the three sts design principles as described above, the collective bargaining system enhances the development of five other principles: joint optimization, redundancy of functions, design and human values, participatory self-design, and incompletion.

In greenfield sites, the ideal of joint optimization of the social and technical subsystems can be more closely approached since social considerations can be explicitly included in the choice of the technology itself as well as the design of the socio-technical system which will operate the technology. However, once in place the technology is usually 'fixed,' at least in the short and medium terms. The flexibility required continuously to redesign the fit between the technical and social subsystems (the principle of joint optimization) resides, for the most part, in the latter (Trist 1981). In most organizations this flexibility is sharply curtailed as key aspects of the social system (e.g., job classifications) are 'frozen' in the collective agreement. In the chemical plant, the collective bargaining system permits and encourages this flexibility. The ideal of joint optimization is, therefore, more fully realized.

The principle of redundancy of functions states that excess capacity should be achieved by building redundant functions into the parts of an organization. The same function can be performed in different ways by using a different combination of parts. There are, therefore, several routes to the same goal. As described in chapter 3, the organization design of the chemical plant reflects this underlying design principle (e.g., multi-skilled workers). The high level of flexibility of much of the chemical plant bargaining system also contributes to making concrete the principle of redundancy of functions. For example, in chapter 4, I described examples of different combinations of individuals and groups being formed to resolve novel problems (e.g., the special grievance process for the redesign of the process operator progression system).

The principle of design and human values states that autonomy and discretion, opportunity to learn and continue learning on the job, optimal variety, social support and recognition, sense of meaningful contribution, and prospects for a meaningful future are basic requirements people have of their work and that jobs and organizations should be designed to fulfil these requirements. However, according to Clegg (1984), much of the job design literature fails to recognize the distinction between tasks and roles, the two principal components of job design. Clegg cites the example of the machine operator in which the task is technologically 'determined,' comprising a number of movements and actions requiring varying degrees of skills. The role includes the decision-making area surrounding the task (e.g., machine set-up, materials control). Clegg concludes that 'there may well be enormous scope for redesigning roles without necessarily changing the technological arrangements especially in the short to medium term ... in the long term both variables are manipulable.' However, much of the scope for role redesign is often embedded in the collective agreement, whose negotiation and administration are the responsibility of representatives, not the workers themselves. Furthermore, in the long run most collective agreements tend to expand not contract, thereby further reducing the scope for role redesign. In the chemical plant the separation of issues between the collective agreement and the GWPH has broadened considerably the scope of role design, thus allowing the principle of design and human values to be enhanced. For example, workers, not union officials, are responsible for vacation scheduling and the overtime system, areas which allow workers to experience variety and develop autonomy and learning.

The principles of incompletion and participatory self-design state that design is a never-ending process and that an organization should be designed by all its members. The inherent flexibility of the chemical plant collective bargaining system permits both the ongoing design of the plant and the direct participation of all workers in the design process. If the items in the GWPH were included in a traditional collective agreement, ongoing design would be at best periodic, and handled exclusively (on the union side) by elected officials. In fact, Davis and Sullivan (1980) doubt if any innovative organization could survive very long without the collective agreement as an enabling and supportive instrument. Furthermore, the team and joint committee structure, a major outcome of the development and application of the philosophy statement, is explicitly designed as the main vehicle for participative ongoing design.

Worker Perspective, Skills, and Norms

The third way in which the chemical plant collective bargaining system and the design principles are linked is more subtle than the first two, but just as significant. The effective functioning of the bargaining system is dependent upon the perspective, skill, and norms developed in the membership by the organization design. Concerning perspective, many of the issues related to administering the GWPH and developing the team and joint committee structure involve part-whole relations. The progression system must be fair to all teams, not just some. Judgments are continually made as to the boundary separating a team issue from a plant-wide issue (e.g., approaches to discipline, co-ordinator roles). The chemical plant is designed so workers develop a perspective on both the part and the whole and their relation to one another. The teams are responsible for the day-to-day running of the whole plant; they receive direct, on-line information about the overall economic effect of particular operating decisions; process operators have a second skill in one of maintenance, the laboratory, or the warehouse, and are multi-skilled in the process area. As a previous local president put it: 'the system forces the appreciation of interdependence both through the jobs and the task forces.'

Concerning skills, the collective bargaining system demands high-level content and process skills. The administration and ongoing design of the progression system, the overtime system, and vacation scheduling, for example, require detailed knowledge of the day-to-day operation of the plant. In addition, along with issues such as the introduction of new technology, they require skills in managing conflict between individuals and groups, problem-solving and decision-making, planning, and communication. These are just the skills developed by the organization design. It is not just that workers receive training in these ares (they do); it is that workers use and develop these skills in their day-to-day work. The skills are so highly developed that according to the plant superintendent, visiting managers from a Shell petrochemical complex in western Canada 'couldn't distinguish the operators from the engineers.' Similarly, the ECWU national director observed: 'A few years ago, we had a meeting with 27 stewards and members at Shell Sarnia and it was one of the most rewarding experiences of my union career. I wanted to know about the human dimension, about how these young people were affected by working in a participative environment. It made such a difference that it shocked me. Each of the 27 could sit down with a problem, analyze it, and develop a solution.'

Concerning norms, the collective bargaining system demands a culture in which taking initiative is commonplace, competence is valued, and the confidence exists to make and remake decisions sometimes under conditions of considerable uncertainty. Without such norms the interactivist (Ackoff 1973) approach to handling the adaptive issues in the third component of the bargaining system could never be developed. This is the culture of the chemical plant, as the following representative sample of quotes illustrates.

'People are willing to take more leadership, responsibility in general and there are more opportunities for this in the chemical plant than in the refinery' [past president of the sister refinery local and member of the initial plant design task force].

'Its ok to be smart around here; if you are you get recognition not flak' [local 800 member with prior work experience].

'People are informed and confident of their knowledge of the situation' [ECWU national official].

'The teams deal directly with head office personnel. The corporate people can't believe their interest, understanding and commitment [internal facilitator].

One significant feature of traditional collective bargaining that is significantly altered as a consequence of the perspective, skill, and norms developed among the members is the relation between indirect and direct representation. In their treatment of labour-management negotiations, Walton and McKersie (1965) assign a full chapter to the problems of the focal position of negotiations, the chief negotiator. The major reason that this role is described as the focal role is that it is the chief negotiator who must accommodate, especially on the union side, the interest, strategies, and tactics of various interest groups. This role, in fact, is said to dominate a large part of the total collective bargaining process. Walton and McKersie argue that the compartmentalization of information and the complexity and novelty of many issues reinforce differences inside the union local. In fact, some issues are judged to be 'too complex to be understood by most members of a union.' The position of the chief negotiator is, therefore, enhanced. Among the tactics listed as appropriate for carrying out this role are such blatantly manipulative ones as:

- limiting membership participation in formulating proposals
- obscuring and misrepresenting the discrepancy between bargaining objectives and results
- limiting membership involvement in the negotiations process
- keeping issues complicated
- silently dropping an issue
- keeping agreements quite
- exaggerating the level of achievement

All of the above reflect and reinforce the dominance of indirect over direct participation in collective bargaining. By contrast, the chemical plant bargaining system, especially the second and third components, reverses this relation. Members are directly involved in the process. Walton and McKersie also list 'directly confronting principals with reality' as a means for involving members in the bargaining process. However, involvement is defined as a tactic for reversing members' expectations in line with those of the chief negotiator rather than a strategy for genuine member participation in the bargaining process.

However, in the chemical plant this direct involvement is only possible given the perspective, skills, and norms developed by the organization design. In turn, the design is a function of the principles of socio-technical systems thinking.

The Future in the Past

I believe the local 800/Shell collective bargaining system to be a harbinger of things to come. However, despite its unique and innovative features, the chemical plant system is not a complete break with, but rather a transformation of, past policies and procedures. The nature of this heritage and of its transformation can be seen by comparing the chemical plants' bargaining system with Strauss's (1978) interpretation of Dalton's classic study of union-management relations in industrial firms in the 1950s, the zenith of scientific management. The focus of Dalton's study was the relation between 'formal' and 'informal' relations, then popular largely because of Hawthorne researches and the studies they stimulated. However, Strauss (1978) has shown that Dalton's data and analysis are, in fact, an excellent (albeit precocious and largely ignored) example of the negotiations approach to the study of organizations:

Organizational theory at the time was picturing such places (industrial firms) as fairly purposeful organizations, their policies developed from above and executed more or less rationally, if not always efficiently, by the echelons below. Dalton's eyes and ears confronted him with a different picture. There was much heterogeneity and clashing of group and individual purpose with people working frequently at cross purposes with little sense of a unitary structure ...

Relations at the plant level, then, are as Dalton puts it, a blur of conflict, co-operation and compromise initiated and guided by cross cliques. The resultant negotiation context understandingly is somewhat complex ... and constitutes a considerable portion of the social order of any of these plants. (122)

According to Strauss, the negotiations observed by Dalton are a continual, unofficial, covert, and 'illegal' set of 'interpretations and practices as union and management try to get around items written into the collective agreement.' In fact, according to Strauss, from the perspective of both union and management contract provisions were seen as 'barriers to getting the work done rather than as helpful for the necessary co-ordination of effort.'

The fact that union and management in Dalton's study persisted in developing an unofficial, covert, and even illegal system of circumventing the collective agreement is strong testimony to the limitations of the traditional contract negotiation and administration. Strauss also points out that the issues handled in the negotiations include complex ones which 'do not necessarily get solved by simple adherence either to long-standing rules or to labour and management identifications.' Finally, the negotiations are characterized by selfish, petty politics. Collusive relations are commonplace. Dalton's writing is full of terms such as 'cheating,' 'cooking the books,' 'prefigured justifications,' 'horsetrading,' 'dealmaking,' 'balancing favours,' 'payoffs,' 'greasing the wheels.' The chemical plant collective bargaining system (in particular the GWPH and its development and administration) has turned Dalton's informal negotiations right side up, acknowledging its critical function and encouraging its development. The unofficial, covert, and illegal has been made official, overt, and legal.

A key feature of the complex issues referred to by Strauss is their novelty. As with the chemical plant, the organizations Dalton studied faced issues which 'involved new areas and putting together combinations of acts and persons that are far from usual.' The fit between the nature of the issues and the structure and process for handling them was further enhanced as the 'working out of differences outside the national contract was not subject to guidebooks or officials' rules, the course of action ... [was] thrown open to the ingenuity of participants.' The similarity to the third component of the chemical plant bargaining system is striking. However, unlike the Shell chemical plant in Dalton's study, this ingenuity is directed towards 'finding means of simulating conformity to the contract while adjusting behaviour to the pressures that could not be escaped.'

The petty political nature of the negotiations described by Dalton and Strauss contrasts vividly with the values expressed in the chemical plant philosophy statement. Indeed, while the latter (as explained earlier) are the basis for adaptive responses to turbulence, the former resemble one of Emery's (1978) three passive maladaptive responses: segmentation. 'Co-production tends to be restricted to the people one knows and can trust. To all intents the social field is transformed into a set of fields each integrated in itself but poorly integrated with each other.' The rationale for the maladaptive approach is hinted at by Strauss: 'implied threat of reprisal lurks behind a great many of the covert and even tacit arrangements.' But it is Dalton (1959) who makes the link with scientific management explicit when he states that all the negotiations are 'essential to prevent the line from revealing staff errors to the top' (104). This quote bears an uncanny similarity to Emery's description of 'normal' behaviour when organizations are designed according to the principle of redundancy of parts, a key principle of scientific management: 'The governing principle of asymmetrical dependence (i.e., redundancy of parts) means that errors will leak in from the environment like water from a sieve. It is in no one's interest to have himself rendered redundant because an error of failure can be associated with him ... Truth will be a precious commodity in an environment where it decays so quickly in transmission up to the key decision makers' (Emery 1978, 93, 95).

One cannot help but speculate that the form of union-management relations observed by Dalton was, in fact, the remnants of a craft union approach to bargaining ravaged and perverted by scientific management. Trist et al (1963) argue that the new paradigm represents the 'loss, rediscovery and transformation of a work tradition' (in fact, the subtitle of their seminal book *Organizational Choice*) which pre-dated scientific management. Accordingly, the chemical plant bargaining system may represent features of a neo-craft form of unionism. Before pursuing this idea In chapter 6, I will examine the critical issue of how local 800 maintains its own interest vis-à-vis management and how it mobilizes members for collective action.

5

ECWU Local 800: Beyond Industrial Unionism

The organization design of the chemical plant undermines traditional union strategies for maintaining an identity and interest separate from that of management and for mobilizing for collective action. The high levels of direct worker participation tend to blur the lines between the two parties. As one member puts it, 'It's hard to separate our issues from their issues.' The enormous diversity of work structures, processes, and practices militates against using uniformity as a basis for building solidarity. However, while the organization design renders old strategies obsolete, at the same time it enables the development of new ones. These new strategies maintain separate interests not by rigidly drawing boundaries between 'us' and 'them' but by continually managing the boundary development process. These strategies develop solidarity not be ensuring the identical treatment of the parts but by continually working through the part/whole relation.

This chapter is divided into three sections. The first elaborates on the misfit between the organization design and traditional union strategies. The second describes several examples of local 800's capacity to maintain its separate interest and effectively act as a collective. The final section, building on the second, elaborates on the four key components of this capacity. These are: the central position the local has taken with regard to the organization design, local 800's innovative structure, the role of elected officials (especially the shop-steward), and the inherent link between the organization design and collective action. Throughout this final section the challenges, tensions, and risks experienced by the union because of the nature of the organization design are highlighted.

The Organization Design and Traditional Union Strategies

The undermining of traditional 'we-they' union strategies for maintaining self-interest and mobilizing for collective action is an inevitable outcome of the chemical plant's collective bargaining system. In this system, the close relationship between union and management has a direct bearing on organization effectiveness. High levels of openness, trust, and support are necessary for administering the GWPH and especially for handling the adaptive issues in the third component of the bargaining system. The low levels of these variables associated with the distributive orientation of the we-they approach to maintaining self-interest would be dysfunctional. In this regard, Walton and McKersie (1965) point out that: 'If information is guarded or patterns of communications confined to a single spokesperson for each side problem solving effectiveness is lowered ... Low trust and defensive atmospheres divert energy from the task at hand, tend to escalate and lead to distortion of facts and opinions; reduce creativity and lower individual's abilities to abstract and reason (142–3). Not only is a close relationship between union and management functional, it is also reinforced by the second and third components of the bargaining system. Walton and McKersie (1965) make just this point in their discussion of integrative bargaining.

During integrative bargaining the parties move closer both substantively and attitudinally. First, because the demands of integrative bargaining require that the parties approach the agenda items from an objective point of view, the interaction can serve to structure positive attitudes between the participants. Under such neutral interactions (as far as attitudinal content is concerned), interaction leads to positive sentiments. Second, to the extent that the parties do more than engage in the interaction and succeed in identifying (or underscoring the salience of) areas of common interest, the participants will tend more to be positively disposed toward each other. (279)

Uniformity, as the basis for solidarity and collective action, is also undermined by the chemical plant's collective bargaining system. Differences among individuals and groups are acknowledged and promoted as they are necessary for the bargaining system to function effectively. Concerning individuals, the handling of certain issues (e.g., the introduction of new technology into the warehouse) often requires the special skills of a particular member. Concerning groups, the redesign of the process operator progression system required the active involvement of an interest group inside the union but outside its formal structure (i.e., operators with prior industry experience who were suffering the most under the old system). Traditionally, in the interest of solidarity such differences would be ignored and even suppressed. The previous chapter referred to Walton and McKersie's (1965) examples of such behaviour in the context of a traditional relationship between a chief negotiator and his/her bargaining unit (e.g., limiting participation in formulating proposals). Such behaviour would be dysfunctional in the context of the chemical plant bargaining system.

Given the impotence of traditional strategies, novel approaches had to be developed by the local to maintain its self-interest and act as a collective. As one president put it, 'we had to figure out new ways of dealing with management – ones that wouldn't screw us.' Some examples of these new ways are described in the following section.

Maintaining Self-interest and Developing Collective Action

On at least five occasions local 800 has aptly demonstrated its capacity to maintain its self-interest and act as a collective. These five are: the inclusion of the right to due process in the collective agreement, the adoption of the initial 12-hour shift schedule, the redesign of the process operator progression system, the refusal to handle the output of a plant under strike by another ECWU local, and the redesign of the craft team progression system. All five have several features in common:

– the insistence by union officials that the development of the organization design is a central union focus

- the effective functioning of the union's flexible, diversified, and decentralized structure
- the role of elected officials in continually working through the boundaries between distributive and integrative issues and between the parts of the local and the bargaining unit as a whole
- the extensive involvement of virtually all the members (either as individuals or through an interest group) in the surfacing of the issue, its definition, the development of the local's response, and its final resolution

I will illustrate and clarify the nature of these features by discussing the redesign of the process operator progression system. Excerpts from other occasions listed will be used to elaborate and emphasize key points in this discussion. The inclusion of the right to due process in the collective agreement and the redesign of the craft team progression system were described in chapter 4. The adoption of the 12-hour shift schedule pitted the local against plant management and the ECWU national representative. They both favoured, for safety reasons, the retention of the 8-hour schedule. The refusal to handle product from a plant under strike is self-explanatory.

The original process operator progression system had to be redesigned because of problems in the plant's technical system. In particular, the time and difficulty in getting the isoprophyl alcohol system to a 'steady state' greatly exceeded that for the polypropylene technical system. As a result many operators were 'stuck' trying to 'get a system up' while others were moving up the progression ladder. In addition, operators with prior industry experience were spending most of their time training others and were hardly progressing at all. Finally, opportunities to practise and develop second skills were severely limited.

As the situation developed, members on their own initiative held meetings (formal and informal) to clarify the nature and extent of the issue. These meetings took place during working hours and included both intra- and inter-team sessions. At the same time the stewards, in meetings chaired by the chief steward, pooled the views of the different teams and took from these meetings back to the teams the views of the executive. A consensus slowly emerged: the progression system was a serious issue, it was a collective issue, the concern was not with the principles underlying the progression system but with their application, and it was a joint union-management issue. 'We, management and union members, have a problem.' By contrast, the inclusion of the right to due process in the collective agreement was defined as solely a union issue; management didn't have a problem, 'they were the problem.'

Once it was established that the progression system was a union-management issue the executive proposed to management that a joint task force be established. Since the issue was seen as a critical collective issue, the union executive insisted it be handled through the union management committee and not the TNRB. The latter represents the different parts of the plan (e.g., the teams) while the former represents the two wholes (i.e., management and union). Furthermore, since in the eyes of the union executive the redesign of the progression system would be 'the most important test for the union and the concept [i.e., the organization design] and we wanted both to survive,' the executive insisted on being directly involved. By contrast, the redesign of the craft team progression system was defined as primarily (but not exclusively) a craft team issue. While a member of the union executive was an initial member of the ad hoc committee charged with redesigning the system, he withdrew once the committee's terms of reference were developed. Even the formal approval of the new craft team progression (as well as its design) was handled essentially by the craft team. (One or two process operators served as technical resources but did not have any final say in the adoption of the new system.)

The union-management committee agreed to form a five-person task force (Three union, two management) to redesign the process operator progression system. The executive then called a general membership meeting to clarify the mandate of the task force, to appoint the union's representatives, and to agree upon procedures for communicating to these representatives relevant information from the members. The president announced that the vice-president and recording secretary would be on the task force and that the final decision (via voting) to adopt a new progression system would rest with the membership as a whole. (Management opposed the idea of a vote, arguing the local executive should be able to speak for the members.) These decisions were 'accepted' without comment given the prior definition of the issue as a collective concern. A general discussion then ensued out of which emerged a consensus that members with prior work experience should be directly represented on the task force. The rationale was twofold: to tap directly their intimate knowledge of the issue and to help ensure their concerns would be thoroughly addressed. Since no one on the executive belonged to this group of workers a vote was held and an appropriate rank-and-file member was appointed. It was then agreed that members would channel their views concerning the nature of the problem and any ideas for its resolution through the stewards.

The joint task force took three months to complete its proposal for the redesign of the progression system. The union members consulted extensively with the stewards and the rest of the executive but during this phase there was little direct contact with members at large. (Several members with prior work experience commented how surprisingly rumour-free this period was.) Once the task force completed the proposal its union members spent a full day reviewing it with the executive and stewards. All the elected officials then held two four-hour meetings with the entire membership clarifying and assessing the terms of the proposal. During this two-stage process explicit attention was paid to the relative financial implications of the proposal for individuals and groups, the feasibility of the suggested procedural changes, and whether the proposal still reflected the values expressed in the philosophy statement. Minor modifications were made as a result of these deliberations. Lastly, the executive organized a vote. There was a turn-out of 100 per cent and the new progression system was approved by a majority of approximately 90 per cent. As described in chapter 4, a special grievance process was set up to handle any remaining complaints. These were all successfully resolved. A similar high level of member support for its representatives was also evident in the refusal to handle the output of plant under strike by another local. Not a single member crossed an information picket line set up by the executive.

The above illustrates the four components of local 800's capacity to maintain its self-interest and act collectively. These are: the central position the local has taken with regard to the organization design, local 800's innovative structure, the boundary management role of elected officials, and the inherent link between the organization design and collective action. In the following section these four components are discussed in detail.

Novel Union Strategies

The Organization Design as a Central Union Focus

A necessary condition for any union to maintain its self-interest and mobilize for collective action is that the union must play a central role in determining the work experience of its members. According to Batstone, Boraston, and Frenkel's (1978) review of the literature, high institutionalized union centrality leads to a mobilization of bias in favour of the union. In cases where union centrality is low, commitment to the union is discouraged and collective power limited. Furthermore, the extent of union centrality is a function of union power. Batstone et al identify the development and maintenance of ideology as the most basic form of power in the workplace. It 'fosters both particular view of the workplace and particular patterns of behaviour ... and those who play a major role in [its] development, if successful, can be seen as having power ... but it has to be continually maintained and reaffirmed' (12).

The design principles and values contained in the philosophy statement make up the ideology that determines structures and processes as well as attitudes and behaviour in the chemical plant. The initial (and ongoing) challenge facing local 800 was to ensure that it was a major architect of this ideology. To aim for anything less in a plant where the entire collective bargaining system (not just some of its parts) was designed according to this ideology would have been tantamount to suicide. Local 800 accomplished this aim by successfully staking out a claim to the new paradigm, a claim independent of and to some extent different from management's. Two developments were crucial to this success: the identification of unions in general and local 800 in particular with some of the key values underlying new forms of work organization and the limiting of the authority of the TNRB.

From the very beginning of its involvement in the chemical plant the ECWU took a strong, proactive position with regard to its design. This position emphasized its 'natural' fit with ECWU policy and practice and the role of the ECWU in its development. According to Stu Sullivan, the national representative who initially serviced local 800: 'When we were approached by Shell we reviewed our constitution, it refers to enhancing the quality of life of our members. The Shell proposal was just an expansion of this but we insisted that the union must play a highly visible, true partner role. This was critical ... we didn't want it to be seen as a company project with the union as a caboose on the train.' This view of the relation between the 'new paradigm' and the ECWU was articulated and strongly promoted by the union's influential national director, Neil Reimer: 'Freedom, democracy and a good life have more ingredients than the wage rate opposite a classification. It is our objective, indeed our duty to play a role in placing some of these ingredients into proper place' (Reimer 1979).

Following the Shell proposal Reimer and Sullivan organized several meetings with the Sarnia area ECWU council to discuss new forms of work organization. In addition, Reimer devoted a considerable portion of the agendas of the 1977 and 1978 annual meetings of all national officials to a discussion of the union's involvement in the Shell chemical plant. At the local level, Reimer and Sullivan took the position that while quality of working life was a new label, its underlying concepts were nothing new and had been promoted by the Oil, Chemical, and Atomic Workers (OCAW) for at least twenty years. In fact, some of the proposed features in the chemical plant, such as progression to the top, 'copied' what the ECWU had bargained for in several other plants. This is not quite true. In other plants, workers in different job classifications were paid according to their qualifications but, unlike the situation at the chemical plant, there was a hierarchy of classifications with access being determined primarily by seniority. With the national officials, discussions about the chemical plant focused on the ongoing need for the ECWU actively to adapt to change. As Reimer put it:

When I became Canadian director of the union in 1954, we were the least likely to succeed. There were at least four other unions in our jurisdiction, and we were the smallest and latest to start. Today the others are all dead, because they failed to meet the challenge. They had a sophisticated management on one hand and sophisticated workforce on the other, but a union that was just reactive. They counted on management to make mistakes, rather than giving leadership themselves.

I have always maintained that to keep a well paid workforce together in a union, they have to provide programs that improve their daily lives. We have the highest industrial wage in the country. Our members don't get too excited about a five percent increase.

They're in a position to look at new relationships, to expect different things from the union. That's why I wanted to establish some new issues to deal with – otherwise we were in trouble. You know what happens to social institutions that aren't in step – there's only 90 members in the flat earth society. And that's why the other unions that started out in competition with us aren't here today. I can't think of any other reason. (Reimer 1980, 20)

After these meetings, the attitudes of the key actors inside the ECWU toward their union's involvement in the chemical plant design ranged from 'wait and see' to strong support. There were no public cases of strong opposition and no one was hostile to the innovations occurring in the chemical plant. While Reimer's personal influence cannot be discounted, many union officials (e.g., Reg Basken, his executive assistant and successor) shared his union philosophy and needed little 'convincing.' As explained in chapter 3, many saw a strong parallel between the principles underlying the chemical plant design and those underlying the structure of the ECWU. In 1981 these attitudes were institutionalized in the form of a policy strongly supportive of QWL initiatives. By that time several locals and national representatives as well as local 800 and its representative were active in developing new forms of work organization. In addition, the ECWU produced a 15-minute video-tape for orienting all new members to the history, structure, and goals of the union. The tape explicitly refers to the sts principles of job design as union goals.

Not surprisingly, the membership of local 800 accepted the position of the ECWU towards the organization design as 'natural.' In fact, for a few of the members without prior work experience there was nothing unusual about either the organization of the plant or the attitude and role of the union. At the local level the connection between the union and 'the concept' was reinforced and institution-alized by the actions taken by the local executive early in the development of the plant and the local. First, the local officially separated from its sister local 848 at the adjacent Shell oil refinery. (Initially, workers at the chemical plant were members of local 848 but had their own collective agreement and membership meetings.) Second, the local amended its constitution to incorporate aspects of the philosophy statement and GWPH. Third, the local (and man-agement) altered the philosophy statement to reflect its joint 'ownership' by union and management while at the same time developing an independent vision of the statement. Finally, the executive organized a special school dealing with the 'concept' and the union. All of these contributed significantly to incorporating the organization design as part of the local union's identity. Con-cerning the establishment of a separate local, the local president at the time stated: 'The members and the executive wanted to really push the work design but in some areas management resisted because of possible implications for the refinery. When I went to the founding convention of the ECWU I had one goal, a separate local. We had taken a vote for independence and everyone agreed. We had nothing in common with the refinery; our contract, working conditions, and work were all different. We wanted to be recog-nized for who we were.'

With regards to the wording of the constitution the president explained that 'Certain parts of local constitutions are uniform across the ECWU. In other parts there is leeway, so in went QWL.' Added another member of the executive: 'We did it [adding word-ing from the philosophy statement and GWPH] because we wanted recognition for its benefits. Management was getting it all; we wanted to emphasize the union's presence.' The philosophy state-ment was altered after the union executive consulted extensively with the teams. There was a general consensus that the original document did not reflect the 'ownership of the concept by the union.' However, convincing management to share ownership was not an easy task. According to a member of the local executive at the time: 'It was just after we formed our own local. We all talked it through and decided that if it was to continue as a real thing it had to be joint. We approached management and said we wanted to change the wording. It was very emotional as to whether it was theirs or ours. We talked for days. At one point Reg [assistant to the national director of the ECWU] was involved. In the end we got what we wanted.'

In addition to joint ownership of the philosophy statement, the local executive worked with members to develop, in the words of the chief steward, 'an alternative interpretation of the statement.' For example, the union's interpretation of semi-autonomous work groups puts more emphasis on the function of these groups in developing self-management than does the company's. The latter tends to emphasize the group's role in enhancing organization effectiveness. By developing an independent view of the philosophy statement, the union, according to one member, enables people 'to see the gaps between theory and practice, the first step in closing the gap.' This is an example of the union exercising what Blackler and Brown (1975) call cultural power,' the control of resources which transform and interpret the values and norms of society' (346). According to Blackler and Brown, cultural power is typically used to limit, not expand, people's view of what is possible, thereby reinforcing the present social organization of society. By contrast, local 800 has seized the opportunity provided by the philosophy statement to expand their member's horizons.

The special weekend school, held in 1981, was organized by the local executive with the assistance of the national representative. It was attended by approximately sixty members including the executive and team stewards. The purpose of this school was to help the local take stock of its experience to date and plan the next steps. A recurring theme in the school was the ongoing need on the part of each generation of the union movement to win freedom. The chief steward compared local 800's challenge of winning the freedom to work without heavy-handed supervision to freedoms won by industrial unions in the first half of the twentieth century as depicted in the movie *The Inheritance*. This film, which was shown at the school, describes the painful birth, struggle for recognition, legacy, and unfinished business of industrial unionism.

The degree to which the local has been successful in establishing the organization design as a central concern of the union is captured in this quote from an interview with Reimer just prior to his retirement in late 1984: 'At first, a lot of people defined it as a management program. But last year, a manager told me it was now defined as a union program. Now we are running with the ball a little faster than some managers want to.'

Building and reinforcing the link between the union and new forms of work organization was one way in which the local developed its central position regarding 'the concept.' The second way was in the design of the Team Norm Review Board. As originally conceived by the union and management (prior to plant start-up) the TNRB was to be the governing body of the plant. It was to have authority to deal with a significant number of plant-wide operational issues, administration, and the audit of team norms for consistency with the philosophy statement. Management was prepared to delegate this authority to the TNRB, which was to be (and still is) made up of representatives of the seven teams, the co-ordinators, one member of the union executive, and one representative from management. The union, however, was not prepared to go this far. According to a management member of the initial design team: 'This was the one real hot issue, whether it would be a recommending or decision-making body. I can recall several long heated sessions. It was a much greater threat to the union than to management. As a matter of fact, putting together our thin collective agreement was easy for them. They were threatened by the T.N.R.B. and we finally backed off rather than come to loggerheads. It became a recommending body only.' This view was shared by a union member of the design team who saw the original role of the TNRB 'usurping the rightful role of the union.'

Once the plant started up, the TNRB was in place, and the first local executive elected, the role of the TNRB was further limited. According to the president: 'The T.N.R.B. was supposed to be the answer to problems in the plant. It was to be the sole power, to take the place of a Union Management Committee. At least in the design that was the idea. In setting up the guide-lines the only difference from a union management committee was that the T.N.R.B. could recommend only. We insisted that it recommend to the Union Management Committee. I was afraid it would take power away from the union as a whole. Even today anything important goes to the Union Management Committee. It is the key regulatory body.'

Over the past several years numerous attempts (none successful) have been made to redesign the role of the TNRB. Management especially has expressed regret that it has never 'lived up to its potential.' During these attempts the union executive has continually resisted pressures (from within itself, management, teams, and individuals) to either disband the TNRB or delegate more authority to it. It would appear that the organization design makes more visible than usual the tension inherent in any organization between the whole and its parts. Consequently, local 800 experiences this tension more acutely than traditional locals. Local 800 has dealt with this tension not by giving into it or suppressing it but by living with it. Along with management, the union has continually monitored the role of the TNRB until an appropriate (but not tension-free) role has emerged. As described in chapter 4, it is a useful forum for identifying issues, gathering data, and mapping out different views. It is capable of handling many issues on its own. But for issues which have to do with integrity of the bargaining unit as a whole (e.g., the process operator progression system) it is appropriately subordinate to the Union Management Committee. The centrality of the union is thus ensured as individual members, teams, and managers go through the union or the Union Management Committee because that is the 'normal way of doing things.'

Establishing the union as central to the members' work experience does not, on its own, ensure the maintenance of an independent position vis-à-vis management or the capacity for collective action. In addition, fundamental innovations were developed in the union's structure.

Union Structure

Local 800's structure both overlaps with and is a response to its environment – the chemical plant organization. By developing an innovative structure the local is better able to deal with the complex issues inherent in the collective bargaining system. As the national representative puts it: 'you can't deal with a new management system with an old union design ... If we ask management to open up their decision making powers and let workers participate in decision making, those members will expect the same from the union.'

At first glance, the structure of local 800 resembles that of most union locals. The bargaining unit as a whole is a key component. For example, the membership as a whole ratifies collective agreements. There is a six-person union executive consisting of a president, vice-president, recording secretary, treasurer, chief steward, and health and safety officer. Elections for the first five positions are held annually; the health and safety officer is elected for a three-year term. All members of the executive are full-time plant operators. The executive, with the assistance of the national representative, negotiates the collective agreement. In addition, as in most locals, there are internal trustees and shop-stewards. The three trustees audit the local's books; they are elected by the total membership every three years. There are seven shop-stewards, one per team. Each steward is elected by his/her team; term of office is left to the discretion of each team. Finally, as required by Ontario provincial law in all workplaces of 20 or more employees, there is a joint union management health and safety committee. (However, local 800 has chosen to take an approach different from that of most locals to the operation of the chemical plant health and safety committee. This approach is consistent with the innovative nature of local 800's structure and is discussed later in this section.)

Despite its superficial resemblance to a traditional union structure, a closer examination reveals that local 800 is much more diverse, flexible, decentralized, and participative. The sheer amount of formal organization within the bargaining units is greater, because in addition to the usual components listed above, the structure includes the seven teams and the elaborate system of joint union-management committees. By contrast, a traditional local does not include formally organized components below the level of the bargaining unit as a whole. Joint committees are few. The teams and joint committees are the points at which the plant organization and the union organization overlap. Unionized members of these groups wear two hats at the same time, that of a member of local 800 and that of a Shell employee. The nature of these groups is a function of management, union, and union-management decisions regarding allocation of authorities.

In local 800, teams have responsibilities normally associated only with union officials, such as shop-stewards. For example, the team, not the steward, represents the union in the first step in the grievance procedure. Also, as was described more fully in chapter four team members and the teams as whole, not union officials, handle, on behalf of the union, most of the day-to-day administration of the issues covered by the GWPH. In a traditional union local structure, teams or work groups as a rule do not have any formal recognition beyond the right to elect a steward. (An exception is skilled trades which in some unions can veto contracts ratified by the majority of membership.)

Within the formal organizational structure of local 800 three basic types of joint union-management committees exist. First, there are permanent committees which meet regularly (e.g., the Team Norm Review Board). Second, there are permanent committees which meet only as required (e.g., the Co-ordinator Selection Review Board). Finally, there are ad hoc committees or task forces (e.g., laboratory organization). More than 25 of these three types of committees have been established since plant start-up.

Committee mandates are often very broad and committees deal with issues central to the chemical plant design and/or the union-management relationship. For example, the following quotation from an internal joint document describes the mandate of the Team Norm Review Board (TNRB): 'As necessary [the TNRB] will review, discuss and provide for resolution of all items pertaining to organization objectives.' A second example concerns the focus of the evaluation task force. This joint committee conducted an in-depth review of the plant's performance, including an exhaustive analysis of its productivity.

A traditional union local would be involved in only two or three joint committees. In fact, a recent study of eight large union locals identified a maximum of two per local (Gershenfeld and Schmidt 1982). Mandates are usually restricted to gathering information and/or advising management. With the exception of health and safety, committees typically deal with issues peripheral to the design and operation of the workplace (e.g., raising funds for charity, plant tours).

The diversity of local 800's structure enables it to be highly flexible. Teams change their representatives on committees if they feel their interests are not being well served. For example, several teams have recalled their representatives on the TNRB. In addition, committee mandates and operating procedures are continually updated, allowing committees to deal with complex changing issues. For example, the mandate and composition of the committee charged with redesigning the warehousing function have twice been changed. Redesigning this function had proved to be a more complicated and challenging task than had first been assumed. Responsibility for an issue is transferred from one committee to another as required (e.g., developing the new progression system was assigned to a task force when the TNRB was unable to handle the issue).

In traditional locals, there is less flexibility. Committee composition usually changes only at fixed election times. Mandates are relatively fixed over time. Few alternatives exist if any part of the structure is not functioning effectively.

Not only is the local's structure diverse and flexible, it is highly decentralized. The decentralization in local 800 is largely a function of the relative power of the teams within the local. Teams sometimes have the power to decide whether an issue will be handled centrally by the executive acting for the local as a whole or by the teams. In one case, management offered team members the opportunity to cover for co-ordinators on vacation, but without extra pay. The local executive, with the backing of the ECWU national office, urged the members to refuse unless the company agreed to pay the extra rate. Two teams agreed with the executive's recommendation but the others accepted management's offers. All teams, whatever their position on this particular issue, argued that it was a team, not a union executive (i.e., total bargaining unit) decision. In the end, some teams even left the decision to individual team members. Another illustration of the relative powers of the team is that they, not just the local as whole, elect representatives to most committees. In Batstone et al's (1978) terms, members through their teams have considerable influence on 'the terms of the debate.' In contrast, in a typical local union, formal decentralization of the responsibilities below the level of the bargaining unit as a whole is almost impossible, given the limited structure of most locals. However, work groups can exercise significant power informally (Kuhn 1962).

The extent of decentralization of local 800's structure is also reflected in the changed role of the shop-steward. In this illustration of the new paradigm, steward responsibilities centre on handling strategic union issues. In traditional locals these issues are handled almost exclusively by the executive. However, as already mentioned, in local 800 many responsibilities which in most locals are assigned to stewards are assigned to teams. The steward is less of a go-between and more of an integrator. A more detailed discussion of the steward role follows later in this chapter.

The union-management committee structure is also an important means of decentralizing power within the local. The most important committee is the Union Management Committee. It is composed of the local union executive, the ECWU national representative, and seven members of management. Its role is threefold. First, it oversees the administration of the collective agreement and the *Good Work Practices Handbook* (GWPH). Second, it ensures the resolution of all issues pertaining to the achievement of the plant objectives. Finally, it audits and promotes adherence to the ideals, values, and principles outlined in the chemical plant philosophy statement. In practice, this means that all committees (e.g., permanent committees and task forces) operate under the direction of the Union Management Committee. The latter defines the mandate and terms of reference of the former. The permanent committees and task forces are made up, on the union side, of mostly rank-and-file members (e.g., overtime equalization committee, performance development task force). In local 800, therefore, members deal with issues which, if addressed at all in a traditional local, would be handled exclusively by union officials.

The most striking illustration of decentralization created by the committee system is the Team Norm Review Board. The TNRB performs two critical functions. It is the second stage in the grievance procedure, and it identifies and addresses many of the problems which affect the entire chemical plant. The TNRB has eleven members, eight from the union and three from management. The eight union members are the local vice-president and one rank-and-file member from each of the process and craft teams. The TNRB operates by consensus. Any member can veto any decision. Such delegation of responsibility and authority is unique to local 800.

The operation of the Joint Health and Safety Committee is another example of the decentralization of power within the local. In most locals, membership on the committee and active involvement in developing programs would be limited to one or two health and safety specialists. In local 800, membership includes the health and safety officer and one rank-and-file member from each of the seven teams. Together with their management counterparts, they develop and administer the health and safety program with an unusual degree of participation from the rest of the plant.

The diversification and decentralization of the local's structure in turn make possible more participation by the members in the affairs of the local than is the custom. The seven teams and the numerous committees, together with the usual general membership meetings and elected positions, increase the number of forums for participation. All workers are, of course, team members. *Ninety per cent* of the membership have participated in at least one committee. In traditional local unions forums for participation are usually limited to membership meetings and a few elected positions. Gershenfeld and Schmidt (1982) found that 84 per cent of the members of traditional locals they surveyed never participated and 7 per cent sometimes participated in a joint committee. However, 30 per cent identified lack of opportunity as the main barrier to their involvement.

Local 800's innovative structure makes for a much different relation than is the custom between elected officials and the membership at large. As one member of the union executive puts it: 'The executive is accountable to the membership on a minute by minute basis. They [the members] expect to participate when they want. If the leaders don't support this kind of participation they're impeached.' A similar sentiment is expressed by the president of a sister local who, after attending a general membership meeting of local 800, commented: 'They all felt they had the right to speak.

Hell! that's no way to run a union'.[1] Not surprisingly, the role of elected officials in local 800 departs somewhat from the norm. This role and the part it plays in developing union self-interest and capacity for collective action form the subject of the next section.

The Role of Elected Officials

Leadership is centrally concerned with the management of boundaries. According to Gilmore (1982): 'Leadership calls for the ability to see the structure of problems and the skills to mobilize the relevant institutional actions. Authority relationships are not prescribed by formal tables of organization, they must be worked out to suit the task at hand ... the creating and dissolution of internal boundaries links the appropriate people to tasks.'

In local 800, this boundary management concern is the major focus of elected officials, in particular the local executive and shop-stewards. The local executive is constantly managing the boundaries between distributive and integrative issues and between the parts and the whole of the union. According to the national representative: 'the executive must protect the rights of the union as a whole without impinging on the rights of the teams and individuals. If not, the teams and members will feel the union is working against them.' This boundary management task is not an easy one. Again, the national representative: 'The executive has to learn a lot of skills, skills you never needed before. In a traditional organization it's nice and simple – the boss is obviously wrong. So the executive hammers the boss and defends the unions position up the line. It's cut and dried. But here, how do you deal with it when it's your own members who are opposing something the union wants? We find ourselves almost playing a mediation role.'

The change in the union's position regarding the addition of a second team co-ordinator is a good example of managing the boundary between distributive and integrative issues. When the second co-ordinator was put in place, despite their anger, the union executive still defined the issue as an integrative one. They proposed the idea of and actively participated in a joint task force to develop ways to use these co-ordinators effectively and phase them out over time. However, once the company raised the possibility of lay-offs among the bargaining unit the executive took a different position. The union refused to participate further in the task force until the company promised that any lay-offs would occur first in the co-ordinator ranks. The company refused to meet this condition. As a result there was no joint union-management activity in this area until management changed their position. Task force activities were then reinstated and the second co-ordinator was phased out.

Managing the boundary between distributive and integrative issues is not without its risks. For example, the executive of local 800 sometimes complain that some members are more attuned to the interests of management that to those of the union. The ECWU, both nationally and locally, is more than willing to confront these risks. According to the national director: 'We hear every ideological argument. Some people say that if workers take on more responsibility, the line between workers and management will be blurred. The way I look at it – if a fellow digs a ditch all his life, his focus won't be blurred. He will know that every morning he has to go out and dig a ditch. But what future is there in that? I can't see relegating 90% of the workforce to a non-participative life just so the line will be clear and no one gets confused.'

The composition of task forces to deal with the process operator and craft team progression system is an example of the executive managing the boundary between the parts of the local and the whole bargaining unit. As described earlier in this chapter, in the case of the former, the issue was defined primarily as a whole bargaining unit issue with the parts of the local (e.g., the teams) being involved but in a secondary role. In the case of the latter, the emphasis was reversed. Managing the boundaries between the teams and the union as a whole is also not an easy task. According to one steward: 'Sometimes people representing their teams forget they're part of a larger body.'

The extent of the inherent tension between the teams and the whole bargaining unit is most evident in the controversy arising out of an incident, early in the life of the plant, in which disciplinary action was imposed (by management) on one member of a team on the recommendation of his peers. The particular action contravened wording in the GWPH. Nor surprisingly, the union executive confronted the team on its behaviour. The latter, however, argued that it was their prerogative to recommend whatever discipline they felt appropriate. This response led to a meeting of representatives of all teams, the executive, and the national representative in which the local's policy regarding discipline was reformulated. Stricter limits were put on team autonomy and with the backing of the executive several teams withdrew completely from any involvement in peer discipline.

As described above the boundary management focus does not deny the need for leadership but instead alters traditional views of the leader-member relation. As one member of the executive put it: 'there is an ongoing sorting out of roles between us and the members. It is not black and white but a different mix depending on the issue.' The second group of elected officials whose main focus is boundary management is shop-stewards. The primary boundary with which they are concerned is that between the teams and the bargaining unit as a whole. This activity is described in detail below. In addition, two other boundary management tasks are briefly discussed.

The steward's major role is to help shape and implement union policies and actions concerning strategic issues. Strategic issues are ones which express and confirm basic principles and directions of the union (e.g., union members working temporarily in management positions, work beyond phase 12 of the progression system).

The major responsibilities undertaken in carrying out this role are:

- providing the local executive, via the chief steward, with a picture of what is happening from the perspective of the teams
- providing the teams, via the chief steward, with a picture of what is happening from the perspective of the executive
- working with the chief steward to integrate the needs and objectives of the teams and the union local as a whole

There is an indeniable and irresolvable tension in the steward role. This tension is a function of the relationship between the part (the team) and the whole (the union). The steward represents both the part in the whole and the whole in the part. She or he must protect the rights and integrity of both. Furthermore, the steward is critical in linking, balancing, and integrating the teams and the union as a whole. This is consistent with Galbraith's (1973) research on integrating mechanisms. He found that in order to cope with high levels of uncertainty and diversity organizations use complex integrating mechanisms including specialized integrating roles. For example, the steward helps determine whether an issue is primarily a team or union responsibility.

One would expect the steward would experience considerable stress in handling this tension, especially given the autonomy of the teams in the union structure. While the role is difficult, it is made manageable for three reasons. First, the steward is not alone in handling this part/whole relationship. The vast majority of team members have been or are involved in committees or task forces which deal with plant-wide issues (often involving tensions among teams and between teams and the whole plant). All process operators also belong to other groups (e.g., warehouse, laboratory). The organization design, therefore, lessens workers' emotional investment in their team and helps them gain a larger perspective than just that of their teams, therefore enabling them to deal with some part/whole problems. Furthermore, the steward is not the only role through which the whole (i.e., the union) is represented in the team. All members of the local executive are also team members. Second, the union, including the steward, in handling part/whole problems uses a working-through approach. As described earlier in this chapter, this approach emphasizes direct member involvement, interest group involvement, flexibility, and the resolution of conflict through expert power and the use of values to guide action. This approach, of course, has been learned and adapted from the team and joint committee structure. Finally, the value-based approach to integrating the parts and the whole reduces the amount of stress involved. This is consistent with Nicholson's (1976) finding that British stewards who adopt a rigid rule-based approach to their role experience significantly more stress than those who adopt a more flexible, general approach. As discussed in chapter 4, flexibility is necessary in dealing with complex issues such as those handled by the stewards.

This working-through approach, of course, characterizes much of the union-management relationship. At times, however, the steward, a few members, a team or teams, or the entire local will use more traditional union tactics in dealing with management. Examples of such tactics are: a steward threatening to embarrass a co-ordinator by exposing aspects of his behaviour which are inconsistent with the plant philosophy to senior management, caucusing as a team to develop a team position prior to meeting the co-ordinator, and the refusal by some teams to handle overtime.

Sometimes traditional tactics are used in combination with the working-through approach. For example, the craft team, at the instigation of the steward, refused after-midnight overtime. This speeded up management's decision to deal with the craft team's issues. The steward, perhaps because of the protection inherent in the position, is often involved when these more traditional approaches are used. In this way the steward helps manage the boundary between the distributive and integrative orientations of the union in its dealings with management.

The steward role in local 800 appears to be different from its counterparts in other locals. Members with prior work experience in unionized settings often describe local 800's steward in such a manner:

'He is not just another boss as in traditional unions.'

'The steward is not used as in other plants; people prefer to deal with issues on their own or through the team.'

'Because of the flexible system on the shop-floor, the people themselves get involved. Things aren't handled by the shop-steward.'

'In a traditional plant, if a member has a problem, the steward knows; here, he may or may not.'

With the centralization of collective bargaining, the role of the traditional shop-steward, especially in the older industrial unions, has been reduced to what Nash (1983) labels 'a manager of discontent – often going through the motions of conflict rather than dealing with its substance' (44). The traditional role is limited to administering the collective agreement by policing management's actions. If and when a contract rule is violated the steward can file a grievance. The inherent limitations of this power were discussed in chapter 2. If at all significant, the grievance is usually handled by a more senior union official.

In local 800, stewards spend little time administering either the collective agreement or the GWPH. As described earlier, the agreement does not deal with issues that need administering on a day-to-day basis. Concerning the GWPH, three reasons account for the low level of steward involvement. First, in both a technical and social sense, the plant is mature. There are few non-routine issues. The rules, guide-lines, and norms in (and outside) the GWPH have evolved to a point where they cover most (but not all) day-to-day situations. They are second nature to most people. Second, the organization is designed to allow and encourage individuals and teams to handle issues that in traditional plants would be handled by an official union spokesperson. The GWPH, for example, is straightforward and written in plain English. It doesn't require shop-floor lawyers (e.g., stewards) to interpret it. Finally, members' problem-solving skills and self-confidence are well-developed; they do not need to rely on 'experts' (e.g., stewards) when handling most day-to-day problems.

It is interesting to note that in local 800 the stewards have significantly more prior work experience than the membership as a whole. They appear to have self-selected themselves or been selected by their peers to steward positions. Because they have more experience, they are in a better position than other less-experienced members to appreciate both the pros and the cons of the chemical plant design.

In the role of steward they can influence member attitudes and union policies and positions. Stewards use this influence to minimize or even keep out the negative aspects of traditional workplaces. They also try to maximize or add to the design the positive aspects of traditional organizations. Finally, when the union is dealing with problems with the design, they attempt to make sure that its unique, positive aspects are not rejected along with the negative. Thus stewards play a major role in managing the boundary between the old and new paradigms.

The Organization Design and Collective Action

Kochan and Verma (1983) argue that in order to understand the actions parties take to make decisions one must 'move from looking at motivational origins and configuration of interests to the distribution of power and resources among the participants' (23). Indeed, as Olsen (1971) and Reynaud (1983) have argued, the existence of a common interest does not necessarily entail the creation of a group for defending it. In the chemical plant the distribution of power is to a certain extent determined by the organization design. In turn this power enables the union to maintain its self-interest and mobilize as a collective.

The link between distribution of power and organization design is established in the literature, particularly the role that formal structures and units designed to aid and formalize decision-making can play in influencing the distribution of power by controlling the information and the criteria or premises used to make decisions. Stevenson, Pearce, and Porter (1985), for example, cite Simon's observation that organizational position largely determines the information and resources available to members, and by implication, formal position gives some actors a great deal more leverage in bargaining situations than others. As described in chapter 3, the organization design of the chemical plant spreads information, makes public decision-making criteria, and allocates significant resources to operators.

From another perspective, Mulder's (1971, 1977) theory of power equalization through participation also suggests how the chemical plant organization design functions in enabling the union to pursue its interest vis-à-vis management. According to Mulder, the more expert is the power possessed by the powerful (e.g., management), and the more the powerless (e.g., worker) participate in decision-making, the greater is the influence of the former. However, in the chemical plant, the perspective, skills, and attitudes developed in the members by the organization design confer on them an expertise which significantly reduces the gap between the two parties. In such cases, argues Mulder, the less powerful will strive further to reduce the gap between them and the more powerful. This argument is born out in the chemical plant. According to the plant's internal consultant: 'Workers spend far more quality time with managers and engineers than they do in traditional plants. They learn about group and organization skills. More important, once they begin to learn these they want to learn more.'

Of particular interest for my study is the link between organization design and *collective* action. Gustavsen (1980) argues: 'When organization of work is of critical importance to the development of activity, it seems to be because work with a reasonable degree of freedom and competence develops and maintains the ability to take initiatives, make judgments and decisions, and make contact with other people to develop joint action. Individual capabilities among workers are primarily of importance to the extent that they improve on the possibilities for joint action and are consequently of primary importance in relation to the collective resources of the workers' (157). Gustavsen's colleague Gardell (1983) supports this line of reasoning. In his review of the Norwegian industrial democracy program (Emery and Thorsrud 1976) he concludes that a work organization that has semi-autonomous work groups as its primary building blocks (as does the chemical plant) improves 'opportunities for contact, support and solidarity between people' and the active involvement in the union by its members. In addition, autonomous groups allow workers to make more visible and integrate the rich personal or tacit knowledge (Polanyi 1962) which, as individuals, they have built up through direct experience in a specific work setting. As Elden (1986) points out: 'Such knowledge is rich with implicit possibilities for action, but remains fragmented and tacit unless systematically brought forth. Workers as individuals have partial and latent explanations related to their work places. Alone, each worker fails to see the whole picture and tends to make incorrect or incomplete attributions of cause and effect – demonstrating "pluralistic ignorance" – and the leads individual "causal maps" to remain isolated, fragmentary, and unused' (244).

Finally, Crozier and Friedberg (1980) argue that groups which can manage their own inevitable conflicts and tensions 'acquire *a collective capacity* of their own which exceeds the capacities of their individual members. With this capacity, they can organize themselves more effectively and/or are more capable of defining and controlling their action' (107; emphasis in original). Managing internal differences, of course, is just the type of skills developed by workers in autonomous groups.

Gustavsen and Gardell's analysis of the link between organization design and collective action is complemented by North American writers concerned with the study of coalitions in organizations (e.g., Williamson 1963; Thompson 1967; Van Velzen 1973; and Bacharach and Lawler 1980). Stevenson, Pearce, and Porter (1985), based on their review of this literature, hypothesize two connections between work organization and the development of coalitions: first, the greater the opportunities for interaction among people, the greater the likelihood of coalition formation; and second, the more discretion people have in carrying out their job responsibilities, the greater the likelihood that they will participate in coalitions. The factors identified by Gustavsen, Gardell, and the coalition writers (e.g, opportunities for interaction, freedom, and competence in the work role) are built into the chemical plant organization design. Indeed, they are necessary for its effective operation. For example, an operator on day shift would typically make task-related face-to-face contacts with 20 to 30 other operators.

To complete the discussion of the relation between the organization design and the local's capacity for collective action it is necessary to deal with one other aspect of the relation. This aspect, while not so straightforward as those discussed above, is certainly just as important. It is the relation between the work organization and the psychic and political dimensions of work.[2] No data were systematically collected on these dimensions. Accordingly, the speculative nature of the following comments must be underlined.

Gilmore (1982), building on the work of Jaques (1955), observes that roles in organizations result from latent functions of containing psychic anxiety as well as rational considerations of division of labour. Jaques is particularly concerned with the function of social structures and processes in reinforcing individual mechanisms of defence against paranoid and depressive anxieties. Because the origins of these anxieties lie in infancy, he argues that organizations display manifestations of unreality, splitting, and other forms of maladaptive behaviour that are typical of infantile responses to anxiety. Menzies (1970), for example, describes how the splitting up of the nurse-patient relationship into discrete tasks helps reduce for the nurse the level of anxiety inherent in a full or total relationship. She goes on to describe how, in order to reduce the anxiety over accepting the responsibilities of her role, nurses split off aspects of themselves from their conscious personalities and project them into others. Of particular significance is the phenomenon of 'upward delegation' in which nurses project some of their most competent parts and assign them to their superiors. Not only do the superiors accept or introject these parts, they in turn vest their incompetent parts in the nurses. The latter's acceptance of these parts accentuates the gap between superior and subordinate. This collusive system is maintained by a formal organization which assigns low-level tasks to highly qualified nurses, making them unnecessarily dependent on their superiors.

In plants, such as the Shell chemical plant, operators 'naturally' experience anxiety about the very real possibility of literally blowing up the plants and themselves. Such a strong objective source of anxiety cannot help but evoke and/or interact with individuals' paranoid and depressive anxieties referred to above. Lawrence (1982), for example, states: 'In any particular organization individuals bring in these anxieties from their inner, fantasy worlds. The chances are that in some organizations there will be real difficulties and dangers such as in nursing, coal mining, and heavy industry or indeed any work situation which has machinery. The individual is always trying to reconcile his inner and outer world and lessen the anxiety of the internal situation. One way this is done is to project the internal situation into current real situations when they symbolize the internal situation' (31).

In traditionally designed chemical plants anxiety is, in part, reduced by splitting up the operator's role into narrow jobs. Operators are concerned about only their small piece of the plant and not the other pieces, let alone how all the pieces fit together. This responsibility is taken up by supervisors, managers, and engineers, who are not only objectively more competent because of their roles, but also idealized by the operators because they carry such an awesome responsibility. The mutual projection and interjection of competent and incompetent parts strengthens this division of labour. As explained in chapter 1, this scientific management approach to the allocating of roles is highly dysfunctional in terms of overall organization performance. Furthermore, while this division of labour reduces anxiety by avoiding responsibility it also enhances anxiety by making operators highly dependent on others.

Lawrence (1982), building on the work of Kets de Vries (1976), maps out the political consequences of this dependency for workers. Compliance and complacency are the manifest behaviours associated with such dependency. Passive individuals become the tools of demagogues. A culture of inadequacy and inferiority develops. Workers turn their anger inward against themselves, withdraw from relations with others, or direct their aggression outwardly through pseudo-independent acts of rebellion. Most adopt either the first or second option, depositing their feelings of hostility onto shop-stewards who are predisposed to the rebellious option. The end result reduces the chance of a 'mature' political relation vis-à-vis management. Instead, according to Lawrence, it

does much to quiten the voice of workers. If the majority of workers could be angry (as opposed to just the minority being 'rebellious') about the conditions that are inducing a sense of nothingness, and loss of self-esteem, they would have either to face their depression (i.e., anger turned inwards) or face why the social structure is as it is. For some, the schizoid position with its pain would have to be considered in order to rediscover how to feel. This would necessitate questioning the myths that abound in the enterprise. As it is, they create a culture that compensates for life at work; a myth system that draws its sustenance from being separate from the culture of management. To question the boundaries of the myth systems would, of course, involve aggression and getting in touch with the latent anger.

Menzies (1960) complements this conclusion, arguing that social systems which require members to incorporate and use primitive defences interfere with people's capacity to deal with external realities. 'The defences inhibit the capacity for creative, symbolic thought, for abstract thought, and for conceptualization. They inhibit the full development of the individual's understanding, knowledge, and skills that enable reality to be handled effectively and pathological anxiety mastered. Thus the individual feels helpless in the face of new or strange tasks or problems. The development of such capacities presupposes considerable psychic integration, which the social defence system inhibits. It also inhibits self-knowledge and understanding and with them realistic assessment of performance' (35). In the Shell chemical plant a 'mature' political relation has developed between local 800 and management. This relation is critical in order for the workers and their union to manage successfully the distributive/integrative boundaries concerning adaptive issues and the part/whole boundaries among themselves.

In local 800 successful boundary management requires an active, confident membership capable of making realistic judgments about the location of boundaries and what lies on either side. Judgments cannot be based on irrational assessments of reality because of worker fantasies about managers as all powerful or all weak, all good or all bad. In local 800, members have a very realistic view of the world. The following quotes, for example, are representative of the views of the relative competence and power of themselves and management.

In the chemical plant you know the bosses better – their strengths and weakness, partly because of the way things are organized. All the information isn't locked up in the engineer's desk. Management even disagrees with each other in front of the workers. You also know your co-workers better, people are not as guarded as what they can do and what they are thinking [a worker with prior work experience].

Around here it's not an audience with God when you meet with the plant manager [another worker with prior work experience].

The basis for this mature political relation is the organization design. Internal psychic and external objective reality are controlled not through scientific management but through the new paradigm. Operators are in control of the whole plant; there is no need to deny their own ability or idealize management. Members resolve their own problems; stewards are not 'trash-cans' of negative feelings. According to the national representative: 'There is less criticism of each other in this local. When criticism is required, it is upfront. Also people are better at accepting it, they are more objective, less defensive.' An important implication of this type of political relation is that appeals to the membership for collective action are not based on emotional oratory (e.g., 'resist evil management' or 'united we can do anything'). While affect is not denied, the tone is much more rational. As the national representative points out: 'There is more analysis and less bullshit in the local. You can't orate your way out of a problem, you can't give a fine speech unless there is real substance to it.'

6 Concluding Remarks

In concluding, I will summarize some of the key findings of the study of local 800 and to discuss their relevance for theory and practice. The chapter is divided into three sections: the first outlines the study's contribution to negotiations theory and the future of unions; the second discusses the limitations of the study; and the third identifies areas of further research suggested by the study.

Contribution to Theory and Practice

Negotiations Theory

As described in chapter 3, negotiations theory suffers from a lack of empirical research. My view of the literature reveals that as a consequence negotiations theory tends to abstract conceptualizations which are not firmly rooted in concrete analysis. My empirical study of local 800 and the chemical plant collective bargaining system contributes to bridging this gap between theory and practice. In particular, this study supports the validity of properties of negotiations identified in the literature. In addition, it identifies two additional properties – flexibility and the dominant form of regulation – and specifies conditions under which exploring the fit between types of conflict and conflict resolution strategies is particularly useful as an analytic tool. Furthermore, the study suggests that the fit between the complexity of issues negotiated and the negotiation structure and process is critical to understanding the process of negotiations. Finally, the study indicates the dramatic impact of the emerging organization paradigm on the nature of negotiations.

The properties of negotiations supported by this study are eight in all. These are the mixed-motive nature of the issues negotiated, the complexity of the issues, the boundaries of the issues, the number of interests, the timing and sequence of the negotiations, the linkages among different sub-negotiation processes, and the visibility of the negotiations to the various interests involved. Table 5 compares these properties with those of the chemical plant collective bargaining system. The comparison indicates that the two sets are very similar but not identical. For example, three of the properties identified in the literature, timing and sequence, visibility, and the existence of sub-negotiations processes, do not appear in the chemical plant set. However, as described in chapter 4, these properties, while not found to be separate, were useful in clarifying the nature of some of the other categories. More important, the chemical plant set contains three additional properties: the flexibility of negotiations, the mode for regulating the issues negotiated, and the dominant form of member participation.[1] It seems unlikely that these three properties are specific to the chemical plant case or even to collective bargaining systems. As argued in chapter 1, flexibility, a value-based approach to regulation and the direct involvement of people, is critical for active adaptation to turbulence – a condition facing more and more organizations.

While the literature states that the fit between types of conflict and conflict resolution strategies is crucial to understanding negotiations, my study suggests the conditions under which this proposition holds and when it does not. As described in chapter 4, when this type of conflict is either distributive or integrative and the issues are of low or moderate complexity, the proposition holds. The fit between the type of conflict and conflict resolution strategy explains the negotiations. However, when the issues are highly complex, it is the fit between this complexity and the resolution strategy which 'better' explains the negotiations.

The third way in which this study contributes to the development of negotiations theory concerns the impact on negotiations of the emerging paradigm of organization. Chapter 4 maps out the critical relation between the sts design principles which underlie the new

TABLE 5
PROPERTIES OF NEGOTIATIONS

LITERATURE	CHEMICAL PLANT
Issues	
Mixed motive	Nature of conflict
Complexity	Complexity
Boundaries	Stability
Structures and Processes	
Number of interest groups	Interest groups involved
Balance of power	Control
Timing and sequence	
Sub-negotiations	
Visibility	
	Flexibility
	Dominant form of conflict resolution
	Dominant form of member participation
	Dominant form of regulation

paradigm and the chemical plant bargaining system. The negotiations literature does not explicitly deal with either the old or the new paradigms. However, Strauss (1978) points out that the 'structural conditions of settings' affect negotiations. As these structural conditions in more and more organizations reflect the new rather than the old paradigm, the nature of negotiations may well change in the manner illustrated in the chemical plant case.

The Future of Unions

The experience of local 800 suggests that unions can successfully adapt at least to the socio-technical version of new forms of work organization. However, as described in this study, adaptation entails a fundamental rethinking of long-established and cherished policies and practices. As discussed in chapter 5, a critical factor in guiding this rethinking is a union vision of new patterns of organization. The development of this vision has barely begun in local 800. Further development will require the efforts not only of other unions but of the labour movement as a whole. A widely shared vision would facilitate agreement about the mission, strategy, and tactics of unions in relation to sts, Japanese management, etc. Such agreement will be necessary if the union movement is to maintain its identity as a *societal* movement as new forms of work organization spread through Canada and the United States.

Central to this union vision must be a rethinking of the relationship between new forms of organization and contract negotiation and administration. The current practice of rigid separation is, as argued in chapter 2, a dead end. It is blocking, not facilitating, unions (and management) moving from the old to the new. The Shell local 800 case is one example of the contract facilitating this transition; others are needed in order to understand better the nature of collective bargaining after Taylorism. One source of ideas in this regard is Sweden, in particular the work of Åke Sandberg (1987) and Pelk Ehn (1988).

The development of a union vision may eventually assist unions in organizing the unorganized, especially workers in so-called team-based organizations. If local 800 is any indication, successful organizing drives will depend on the union's ability to define as central its formative role in enhancing the positive aspects of new forms of work organization as well as its traditional role of defending workers against incompetent or unjust management. In this regard, the ECWU has drawn heavily on its experience in the Shell chemical plant in developing its current campaign to organize a nearby 'greenfield' plant which is designed according to sts principles.

Relative to their counterparts in the United States, Canadian unions are in a much better position to respond to the challenges of new forms of work organization. In Canada, membership in unions has been slowly increasing over the past few years and currently stands at close to 40 per cent of the non-agricultural workforce. By contrast, U.S. unions have experienced a dramatic decline in membership from 35 per cent in the mid-1950s to 19 per cent in the 1980s (Kochan, Katz, and McKersie 1986). In addition, public attitudes towards organized labour and labour legislation (despite serious shortcomings) are generally more favourable in Canada than in the United States. Consequently, in the United

States new forms of work organization have been, and will continue to be, developed (with some exceptions) solely on management terms. In Canada, in many sectors of the economy unions are too strong to be ignored. Canadian unions, however, are not strong enough to achieve (at least in the short run) legislative changes in areas such as employment security (especially in relation to new technology), access to management information, and the scope of bargaining. Such changes would help to create some of the conditions necessary for an ideal joint approach to the development of new forms of work organization. It may be possible, though, for particularly strong unions such as the CAW to negotiate 'good enough' conditions through collective bargaining. This appears to be the case in the United States with the General Motors UAW Saturn project.

A more realistic strategy for Canadian unions is to collaborate with management in areas where the interests of the two parties overlap and are more or less compatible, and where the union is willing and able to work both independently and jointly with management. Essentially this has been the strategy of the ECWU, not only in the Shell chemical plant but in several other locations as well. In deciding how to engage with management, a sector-based approach may prove to be the most effective, since it overcomes some of the limitations of relying exclusively on activities at either the enterprise or the societal level, or both. On the one hand, the development of new forms of work organization raises issues which cannot be dealt with solely at the level of enterprise (e.g., training and education) and tends to isolate individual locals (e.g., local 800). On the other hand, the societal level is often too distant to engage labour and management or to make effective policy and program decisions. Witness the demise of the Ontario Quality of Working Life Centre and the ongoing difficulties of the Canadian Labour Market and Productivity Centre.[2]

Limitations of This Study

There are four significant limitations to generalizing the study findings beyond local 800. First, and foremost, is the sample size – one. The other limitations have to do with certain characteristics of the membership of local 800: size, diversity, and selection bias. This section discusses the significance of these limitations and suggests how they might be overcome in future studies.

Sample Size and Membership Size, Diversity, and Selection Bias

In chapter 3, I described local 800 as a 'leading part' (Emery and Trist 1973). Certain features of the plant setting and design – a greenfield site, continuous process technology, semi-autonomous work groups, and the organization-wide scope of the design – make this case of particular significance for exploring my study topic. However, a single case is not sufficient to generalize the study findings. More cases are required in order further to develop my interpretation of the experience of local 800. In developing this interpretation, however, the goal of building an all-encompassing theory is not worth pursuing. According to Gustavsen (1983b), 'It is not possible to develop general theory which stands in a one-to-one relationship to specific workplaces ... instead general theory should be limited to main ideas and concepts which can function as inputs or building blocks into processes of local understanding and local theory building.' In particular, it would be useful to examine the experiences of local unions which, unlike local 800, have negotiated contracts guaranteeing union involvement in strategic business decisions.

In addition to sample size, the size, diversity, and selection bias of the membership of local 800 limit the extent to which one can generalize the study findings. A bargaining unit of 160 is significantly different in structure, process, and culture from one of several thousand. In the latter, for example, the opportunity for face-to-face contact among the membership is severely limited. It will be important, therefore, to monitor the experience of the UAW in General Motor's new Saturn plant. According to initial reports (*Business Week*, 5 August 1985) this plant will have a highly advanced socio-technical design and will employ approximately 6,000 workers.

The second limitation of the study inherent in the make-up of the membership is its small degree of diversity. The relative homogeneity of local 800 members in terms of age, sex, education, language, and ethnic origin makes integration less problematic than in many work settings. The diffusion of the socio-technical approach to organization design into sectors with a more diverse workforce (e.g., government and service) should make it possible to clarify the significance of workforce diversity.

The final limitation of this study has to do with the selection of the original 160 members of the bargaining unit. These members were selected from over 2,500 candidates. It is possible, therefore, that local 800 is composed of an élite group of workers who are not representative of the general population. However, it is interesting to note that Shell's new oil and gas complex in Scotford, Alberta – the largest of its kind in the world – is staffed entirely by long-term Shell employees. These employees, many with more than twenty years' service, have transferred to Scotford as Shell closed several money-losing refineries across Canada. According to the internal consultant, the Scotford complex is 'more advanced from a socio-technical design perspective than Sarnia, yet the workforce is more than able to adjust.'

Suggested Further Research

The above discussion of the limitations of this study identifies several important areas for further research. These all have to do with examining the effect on unions of new patterns of organization in different settings. Ideally, such studies should focus on each level and combination of levels of the union organization. In addition, this study suggests two other research topics: the effect of unions on the emerging paradigm of organization, and the extent to which local 800 is indicative of a neo-craft form of unionism.

Mansell (1987a), in her review of the Canadian experience with new forms of work organization, suggests that certain aspects of the new paradigm are different in a union than in a non-union setting. For example, in the former, differences of perceptions may be defined as differences of interests, and individual problems as collective problems. Mansell goes on to suggest that a full expression of the new paradigm may not be possible in a non-union setting because without an independent worker power base (e.g., a union), workers' interests cannot be fully represented. Accordingly, the extent to which the ideal of joint optimization of an organization's social and technical systems can be approached is significantly limited. Similarly, Kochan, Katz, and McKersie (1986), based on their assessment of the American experience with new forms of work organization, argue that if connecting these new forms to more strategic business decisions is necessary for their survival then 'a strong union presence and active support for the process are also essential. Non union forms or those with weak unions are unlikely to develop or sustain this full form of worker participation' (176–7).

Another possible effect of unions on the new paradigm, enhanced organization effectiveness, is suggested by the Shell case. While several studies (e.g., Nightingale 1982) have shown a link between productivity and more democratic forms of work organization, one may speculate that in the Shell case, plant performance (e.g., throughput levels reaching 195 per cent of design capacity) is also related to the unions' role in managing the relationship between individuals, teams, and the workplace as a whole. Effective handling of this relationship is no doubt necessary to maintain worker involvement in a 'high commitment' organization. Perhaps the presence of a union, which at least makes collective issues visible, improves the handling of this relationship.

One way to explore the effect of unions on the new paradigm is through comparative research. A comparison between the Shell Sarnia plant and Shell's non-unionized Scotford refinery would be particularly fruitful. Both are 'greenfields,' use a continuous process technology, and, of course, belong to the same parent company. In addition, the innovative design of both facilities is plant-wide and includes semi-autonomous groups.

In chapter 1, I discussed how the emergence of scientific management as the dominant form of work organization had spelled the 'end' of craft unionism and gave birth to industrial unionism. The experience of ECWU local 800 suggests that as the new paradigm of organization supplants the old, yet another form of unionism may be emerging. The nature of this new form may have been foreshadowed in the subtitle of *Organizational Choice* (Trist et al 1963). *The Loss, Rediscovery and Transformation of a Work Tradition* referred to the miners' transformation of Taylorism through adapting and applying their collective experience with a pre-scientific management or craft-like form of work organization. This neo-craft form of work organization, as described in chapter 1, has since been further developed and labelled as the new paradigm of organization. ECWU local 800 may, therefore, indicate the beginnings of a neo-craft form of unionism.

At first glance there appear to be strong similarities between craft unions and ECWU local 800. For example, Piore and Sabel (1984) include worker and manager collaboration in the ongoing development of the production process as a central feature of craft unions. Such collaboration is, of course, a dominant aspect of local 800's role in the Shell chemical plant.

Care must be taken in adopting the idea of a neo-craft form of unionism. However, there are also some distinct differences between craft unions and local 800. For example, for craft unions the apprenticeship program was central to ensuring the developing of highly trained (and highly paid) craftsmen. While some ongoing training was required to maintain this skilled position, it was secondary to the initial period of apprenticeship, which could extend for several years. Accordingly, craft unions concentrated on regulating apprenticeship programs. However, for today's unions technological change is continually blurring the boundaries between crafts, and between craft and semi-skilled and even managerial work (Rosenbrock 1983). Therefore, new concepts of skill are required and the capacity for ongoing learning is becoming more important than prior training (Hirschhorn 1984).[3] This shift in emphasis is evident in the case of local 800, where the ongoing redesign of the progression system consumes much of the union's energy and where social skills (e.g., communication, negotiation) are critical. It may well be that the notion of neo-craft unionism is misleading, as it draws our attention to more familiar, and possibly less significant, features of the emerging form of unionism. By contrast, Heckscher (1988) identifies this new union form as associational unionism, highlighting its emphasis on a wider range of issues and employees than is usual in industrial unionism.

Significant research and practical action concerning the above issues are perhaps best considered as long-term processes, as traditional ways of thinking about unions, labour, management, and the economic foundations of society continue to undergo profound changes in the post-Taylorist age. It has been suggested that these changes do not bode well for organized labour. But while the future cannot be predicted, the experience of ECWU local 800 in shaping new forms of work organization offers hope for a more democratic workplace.

Collective Agreement between Shell Canada Products Limited and the Energy and Chemical Workers Union Local 800

Effective February 1, 1988, to January 31, 1990

Foreword

The purpose of the agreement which follows is to establish an enabling framework within which an organizational system can be sustained that will ensure an efficient and competitive world-scale Chemical Plant operation and provide meaningful work and job satisfaction for employees. Recognizing that there are risks involved and that there are many factors which can place restraints on the extent to which changes can occur, both Management and the Union support and encourage policies and practices that will reflect their commitment to the following principles and values:

employees are responsible and trustworthy, capable of working together effectively and making proper decisions related to their spheres of responsibilities and work arrangement – if given the necessary authorities, information and training.

employees should be permitted to contribute and grow to their fullest capability and potential without constraints of artificial barriers, with compensation based on their demonstrated knowledge and skills rather than on tasks being performed at any specific time.

to achieve the most effective overall results, it is deemed necessary that a climate exists which will encourage initiative, experimentation, and generation of new ideas, supported by an open and meaningful two-way communication system.

Recognition

The Company recognizes the Energy and Chemical Workers' Union Local 800 as the sole bargaining agency for all multi-skilled operators (hereinafter referred to as Shift Team Members) and journeymen and craft trainees (hereinafter referred to as Craft Team Members) of the Shell Sarnia Chemical Plant at Corunna, Ontario.

The provisions and intent of the Collective Agreement, and those items jointly developed in the Good Work Practices Guidebook, along with the principles and values of the Philosophy Statement form the foundation for all activities at the plant.

Both parties agree to joint consultation on changes to practices and conditions developed between the parties.

Plant Committee

The Company acknowledges the right of the Union to appoint or otherwise select a plant committee. This committee, on behalf of its membership, will be responsible for the negotiating of revisions to the collective agreement where applicable or any other matter which may be mutually agreed between the parties.

The Company agrees to recognize one (1) steward from each shift team and in addition one (1) steward from the craft team.

Grievances

There has been developed, documented and will be maintained a system to ensure the prompt and equitable resolution of problems at the Chemical Plant. In any event, to augment this system the appropriate provisions of the Ontario Labour Relations Act are available to the parties.

Hours of Work and Rates of Pay

All employees covered by this agreement will follow appropriate work schedules that provide for an average basic work week of 37-1/3 hours.

Where circumstances require shifts or schedules other than those in common use, discussion between Management and the Union prior to implementation will occur.

Where a schedule change occurs as per the above whereby the starting or stopping time of an employee is altered by four hours or more, of his/her days off are changed, the employee will be paid, in addition to his/her regular salary, a premium payment of straight time on the first day of his/her new schedule, and his/her days off will become those shown on the new schedule. If an employee works more than 672 hours within a 126-day cycle as a result of a change of schedule exclusive of overtime, the additional hours will be paid at the premium rate. If a change of schedule occurs on a statutory holiday, the premium rate for the change of schedule will be paid on the first day worked on the new schedule, immediately following the statutory holiday.

All overtime hours will be paid at double time.

A minimum payment for call-out work will be equivalent to four hours regular pay, except where, with previous notice, an employee starts to work two hours or less before commencement of his/her regular working day.

In addition to the regular monthly salaries outlined in Schedule "A", shift team members while on the shift portion of their work schedule (i.e. on that part of the schedule which requires them to work on a rotating two 12-hour shift basis) shall receive a "shift bonus" as follows:

A) Hours worked on day shift (7:00 a.m.–7:00 p.m.) – 3.00%
B) Hours worked on night shift (7:00 p.m.–7:00 a.m.) – 5.67%

Under no circumstances will shift team members assigned to a regular or temporary day shift schedule or assignment receive the premium in (A) above. Additionally, shift team members on the day assignment portion of their work schedule or when employed on overtime, practising their second skill, will not be eligible to receive the premiums above.

Team members who are placed on a schedule that begins before 6:00 a.m. or ends after 6:00 p.m. will receive 5% of their equivalent hourly rate for each hour worked between 4:30 p.m. and midnight, and 6% of their equivalent hourly rate for each hour worked between midnight and 8:00 a.m.

Twelve-Hour Shifts

The continuous 12-hour rotating shift schedule will continue providing they result in no increased costs to the Company, and no reduction in operating efficiency. Guidelines for 12-hour shifts and overtime coverage have been developed and documented in the Good Work Practices Guidebook. Each party may at any time elect to revert to the former 8-hour shift schedule by giving the other party 60 days' notice in writing.

Deductions of Union Dues

The Company will deduct from all employees covered by this agreement an amount equal to the regular monthly dues of the Union and remit the amount deducted, together with an itemized list, to the Secretary-Treasurer of the Union. Two changes in the deduction of dues in any calendar year, as notified by the Secretary-Treasurer of the Union, will be permitted.

Seniority

Seniority shall refer to continuous service at Shell's Sarnia Chemical Plant, and for the purpose of establishing seniority of employees at Shell's Sarnia Chemical Plant, the first day of operation shall be deemed to be March 1, 1978.

Severance Pay

(a) *Permanent Work Force Reduction*
In the event of technological change, or the permanent closure of all or part of the plant which, in the opinion of the Company, will result in a permanent work force reduction, the Company will:
1. Notify the Union six (6) months in advance; and,
2. Meet with representatives of the Union to discuss the impact of the change on the work force.

If after using attrition, reduction in the work force is unavoidable, terminated employees will be entitled to severance pay, provided:.
1. the employees have not refused to exercise seniority rights to claim other available jobs within the bargaining unit;
2. the employees have not rejected reasonable alternative employment which the Company may offer to the employees;
3. the employees remain available for work until the designated date of termination; and,
4. the employees, by virtue of performance or actions prior to or during the notice period of termination, are not discharged for just cause.

Severance pay will be calculated on the basis of one (1) week's pay per year of service. For the purpose of this calculation, a week's pay is defined as 37.3 hours pay at the employee's straight time basic wage rate at the time of termination. Partial years of service will be prorated for the calculation of severance payments and such payments will be subject to statutory deductions.

Should the Company be required by law or otherwise to make any payments by reason of layoff or termination of any employee exclusive of:
– earned vacation
– pension payments
– sickness or disability insurance payments
– workmens' compensation
such payments shall be deducted from the severance payment provided for herein.

(b) *Layoffs Due to Lack of Work*
In the event of a layoff, reverse-order seniority will be followed, provided that remaining employees are capable of fulfilling all job requirements.

In the event of a layoff due to lack of work for a continuous period which exceeds six (6) months, the laid off employee will be terminated and be entitled to severance pay as provided in (a) above.

(c) *Recall*
Employees laid off due to lack of work retain recall rights for a period of six (6) months from date of layoff. Recall shall be in accordance with plant seniority, subject always to the same provisions as outlined in (b) above.

Vacations

Every employee covered by this agreement will have the following vacation entitlement:

Completion of one full years' service
    – three weeks' vacation with pay

Completion of ten consecutive years' servics
    – four week's vacation with pay

Completion of twenty consecutive years' service
    – five weeks' vacation with pay

Completion of twenty-five consecutive years' service
    – six weeks' vacation with pay

Statutory Holidays

Days designated as Statutory Holidays are as follows: New Year's Day, Good Friday, Victoria Day, Canada Day, Civic Holiday, Labour Day, Thanksgiving, Remembrance Day, Christmas Day and Boxing Day. In addition, every regular employee will be entitled to an 11th statutory holiday, to be taken as a personal floater, subject to the guidelines contained in the Good Work Practices Guidebook.

Statutory holiday pay and pay for work performed on a statutory holiday are distinct and separate. Team members required to work their regular shift and/or overtime on a statutory holiday will be paid at double time their regular salary rate in addition to receiving their 8 hours statutory holiday pay.

Health and Safety

The Company agrees that the Union, in consultation with team representatives, may appoint two representatives on the Health and Safety Committee, and that these representatives shall be notified in advance of meetings of this committee which have been called for purposes of Health and Safety or to investigate accidents involved in injury to employees.

Termination

This agreement shall remain in force for a period from the 1st day of February, 1988, up to and including the 31st day of January, 1990, and shall continue in force year to year thereafter unless in any year not more than 120 (one hundred and twenty) days, and not less than 30 (thirty) days, before the date of its termination, either party shall furnish the other with notice of termination of, or proposed revision of, this agreement.

Schedule "A"
BASIC MONTHLY SALARIES
February 1, 1988 & February 1, 1989

	Feb. 1, 1988	Equivalent Hourly Rate	Feb. 1, 1989	Equivalent Hourly Rate
SHIFT TEAM MEMBERS				
Phase 12	$3,451	$21.28	$3,606	$22.23
Phase 11	3,342	20.60	3,492	21.53
Phase 10	3,231	19.92	3,376	20.81
Phase 9	3,128	19.28	3,269	20.15
Phase 8	2,995	18.46	3,130	19.30
Phase 7	2,858	17.62	2,987	18.42
Phase 6	2,756	16.99	2,880	17.76
Phase 5	2,647	16.32	2,766	17.05
Phase 4	2,540	15.66	1,654	16.36
Phase 3	2,432	14.99	2,541	15.67
Phase 2	2,325	14.33	2,430	14.98
Phase 1	2,250	13.87	2,351	14.49
CRAFT TEAM MEMBERS				
Journeyman	3,194	19.69	3,338	20.58
Craft Phase 5	2,975	18.34	3,109	19.17
Craft Phase 4	2,756	16.99	2,880	17.76
Craft Phase 3	2,647	16.32	2,766	17.05
Craft Phase 2	2,486	15.33	2,598	16.02
Craft Phase 1	2,325	14.33	2,430	14.98

Good Work Practices Handbook

Table of Contents

SECTION 1 – HOURS OF WORK & SCHEDULING
1.1   Hours of Work
1.2   Twelve-Hour Shifts
1.3   Progression System
1.4   Change of Schedule
1.5   Shift Differential
1.6   Shift Team Members Hired in Mid-Cycle
1.7   Shift Team Members Terminating in Mid-Cycle
1.8   Changing of Second Skill
1.9   Mutuals
1.10 Vacations
1.11 Statutory Holidays
1.12 Floating Holiday
1.13 Leaves of Absence

SECTION 2 – OVERTIME
2.1   Overtime
2.2   Overtime Distribution
2.3   Overtime Meals

SECTION 3 – ROLES
3.1   Role of the Shift Team Coordinator
3.2   Role of the Craft Team Coordinator
3.3   Role of the Team Steward
3.4   Role of the Union/Management Committee
3.5   Role of the Team Norm Review Board

SECTION 4 – HEALTH & SAFETY
4.1 Safety and Security
4.2 Safety Glasses
4.3 Safety Shoe Program
4.4 Nomex Work Clothing Program
4.5 Damaged Clothing Policy
4.6 Occupational Health Centre
4.7 Alcoholism and Drug Abuse
4.8 Tours for Friends, Relatives, etc.
4.9 Photography
4.10 Parking
4.11 Driver's Licenses
4.12 Gate Passes

SECTION 5 – EMPLOYEE RELATIONS
5.1 Employee Relations
5.2 Personal Information/Benefits
5.3 Employment Agreement
5.4 Veba-Chemie Isopropanol Technology Confidentiality
5.5 Performance and Development Review

SECTION 6 – SPECIAL PROGRAMS
6.1 Shell Employees' Recreation Association
6.2 Educational Training Plan
6.3 Physical Fitness Program
6.4 Shell Employees' Community Service Fund

SECTION 7 – MISCELLANEOUS
7.1 Paycheques
7.2 Problem Resolution Procedure
7.3 Compressor Certificates
7.4 Out-of-Town Training Assignments
7.5 Bulletin Boards

ADDENDUM – ORGANIZATION NORMS

Sarnia Chemical Plant Philosophy Statement Related to Work Design

The primary objective Shell Canada Limited represented by all employees at the Sarnia Manufacturing Centre Chemical Plant is to obtain an optimum return on investment in capital and human resources, operating in a safe environment as a responsible member of the community, while being responsive to employees needs. It is believed that this objective can best be achieved by establishing and sustaining an organization and management system consistent with the following philosophy.

I Social and Technical Interactions

Employees recognize that, in order to achieve the primary objective, it is necessary to give appropriate consideration to the design and management of both the social and technical aspects associated with the Chemical Plant operation. The former is related to employees and encompasses such areas as organizational structure, levels of responsibility and authority, supervisory roles, communication networks, interpersonal relationships, reward systems, etc. while the latter deals with the physical equipment – its capacity layout, degrees of automation, etc. Although our operations involve a high degree of sophisticated technology which can be exploited to improve efficiencies, it is only through the committed actions of employees that the full benefits can be realized. The social and technical systems are inter-related and must be jointly taken into account to achieve overall optimization.

II Key Considerations for the Social System

Communications: Our operation is a highly integrated system, functioning on a 24-hour 7-days-a-week basis, with associated support activities carried out on a weekday schedule. Involved are people at various levels and widely dispersed in locations both inside and outside the plant. The nature of our industry is such that delay in recognizing errors or need for operational changes, and taking corrective actions, is likely to result in substantial cost. Considerable consideration must, therefore, be given to design and maintenance of a communication network that avoids lapses of attention and errors in observing, diagnosing and communicating or acting upon information. Accordingly, information should be directed to the individual capable of acting most promptly and for that individual to have authority to take action and to be internally motivated to do so.

ii) *Individual Commitment*: An essential ingredient for the success of our operation is a high level of individual employee commitment. Such commitment, however, can only be expected to develop if, in addition to provision of satisfactory working conditions and terms of employment related to remuneration and benefits, other needs such as the following are met:

1. The need for the content of the work to be reasonably demanding of the individual in terms other than those of sheer endurance, and for it to provide some variety.
2. The need for an individual to know what his/her job is, how he/she is performing in it, and how it relates to the overall objectives of Shell Canada Limited.
3. The need to be able to learn on the job and go on learning.
4. The need for some area of decision making where the individual can exercise discretion.
5. The need for the individual to know that he/she can rely on others in time of need and that his/her contribution is recognized.
6. The need to feel that the job leads to some sort of desirable future.

The relative significance of these needs vary [sic] from individual to individual and it is not possible to provide for their fulfilment in the same way for all people. It is also recognized that different jobs will provide varying degrees of opportunity for the fulfilment of particular needs. Allowance must, therefore, be made to accommodate individual differences.

III Implementation and Maintenance of the Philosophy

1. In developing a social system within our plant, the following are regarded as key criteria to be incorporated:
   Policies and practices should reflect the belief that:
   i. Employees are responsible and trustworthy.
   ii. Individuals are capable of making proper decisions related to their sphere of responsibility, given the necessary information, training and authority.
   iii. Groups of individuals can work together effectively as members of a team with minimal supervision, collaborating on such matters as problem

solving (operational and personal), training, "hands-on" operations, maintenance, etc.

2. Employees should be permitted to grow, advance and contribute to their fullest potential and capability.

3. Compensation should be on the basis of knowledge and applicable skills, rather than the task actually being performed.

4. Communications should be open and meaningful. Direct communications across departmental boundaries between specific individuals concerned, without passing through intermediaries, is most effective.

5. Information flow should be for the purpose of ensuring that the most expeditious action is taken on the basis of that information, and should, therefore, be directed to those in a position to most quickly act upon it. Disemination of such information to others should be only for purposes of appropriate audit and not for the purposes of decision making and exercise of control.

6. "Whole jobs" should be designed, so that individuals are involved from start (premises, conception, economics, etc.) to end (evaluation of results).

7. Systems should be designed to provide direct, immediate feedback to the individual of the results of his/her actions in meaningful terms, to the fullest extent possible.

8. Work should be designed to permit employees a maximum amount of self-control and discretion. They should be given authorities commensurate with position and held personally accountable.

9. A system should be developed which permits any employee to undertake any task required for the efficient operation of this plant, provided he/she has the skills to do the work effectively and safely. Artificial, traditional departmental or functional demarcation barriers should be eliminated to the extent possible and work allocated on the basis of achieving most effective overall results. The training and remuneration programme must be designed accordingly.

10. Jobs should be designed and work schedules developed to minimize time spent on "shift."

11. A system and climate must be established for early identification of problem areas with problem solving occurring in a collaborative fashion.

12. It is necessary to have a climate which encourages initiative, experimentation, and generation of new ideas. Error situations should be reviewed from a "what can we learn" standpoint and not from a punitive one.

13. Status differentials should be minimized.

It is recognized that bringing about change in an on-going operation is an extremely difficult task which must be approached realisitically and patiently, because we are dealing with deep rooted attitudes and practices. The most promising opportunities lie in "grass roots" circumstances. Building a new facility adjacent to an existing one does not necessarily require that the practices of the older operation be extended to the new installation. Indeed, the new installation provides an opportunity to introduce changes to the older organization.

There are many factors which place restraints on the extent to which the above criteria can be embodied in the various organizational systems. Our task will be to properly examine all our practices and determine strategies for overcoming these obstacles.

Summary

1. a) Employees are responsible and trustworthy.
   b) Employees are capable of making proper decisions given the necessary training, information and authorities.
   c) Groups of individuals can work together effectively as members of a team.
2. Advancement and growth to individual's fullest potential and capability.
3. Compensation on the basis of demonstrated knowledge and skill.
4. Direct, open and meaningful communications amongst individuals.
5. Information flow directed to those in position to most quickly act upon it.
6. "Whole Jobs" to be designed to provide maximum individual involvement.
7. System that provides direct and immediate feedback in meaningful terms.
8. Maximum amount of self-regulation and discretion.
9. Artificial, traditional, or functional barriers to be eliminated to the extent possible.
10. Work schedules that minimize time spent on shift.
11. Early identification of problems and collaboration on solutions.
12. Errors reviewed from "what can we learn" point of view.
13. Status differentials to be minimized.

Notes

Chapter 1

1 According to Merkle (1980), the world-wide diffusion of this paradigm transcended political and cultural barriers.

2 For ease of reading, the terms 'old paradigm of organization,' 'Taylorism,' and 'scientific management' are used interchangeably. From a social science point of view, this is not strictly correct.

3 However, the overall strategy of unions in the garment industry, both today and in the past, is quite consistent with the emerging form of unionism suggested by ECWU local 800.

4 Pava (1986a) points out that the traditional sts design methodology, developed in industrial settings, is ill-suited to the non-linear, multiple conversion work processes which often characterize service organizations and proposes an alternative methodology. However, Pava maintains that the core sts concepts are still appropriate for understanding non-industrial settings.

5 Critics of the sts approach (e.g., Kelly 1978) have argued that there have been very few examples in the sts literature of technology being changed to accommodate the social system. Leaving aside Kelly's failure to distinguish between technology and technical system, recent developments, such as the new Saturn and Volvo Uddevalla assembly plants, suggest that his observation was valid for a very limited time period.

6 Joyce Ranney points out that the sts approach lacks rigorous methods and techniques for pursuing continuous design or improvement. She suggests that some of the tools found in the Total Quality field (e.g., design of experiments, quality function deployment) might help overcome this weakness.

7 My treatment of industrial unionism, scientific management, and the new

paradigm of organization owes much to my colleague Wayne Roberts. Many of the ideas presented here were developed during numerous discussions between Wayne and me while we were both employed at the Ontario Quality of Working Life Centre. In addition, I have drawn heavily on his unpublished 1984 paper 'Lots of Um's: Collective Bargaining and Industrial Democracy.' Rather than break the flow of the text by continually acknowledging his contribution, I have cited his works on only a few occasions. These citations on their own do not reflect the extent of his contributions. Ultimately, of course, any biases or errors are mine.

8 An excellent, if perhaps extreme, example is included in Commons's description of the meat-packing industry (quoted in Griffin, Wallace, and Rubin 1986): 'The animal has been surveyed and laid off like a map; and the men have been classified in over thirty specialties and twenty rates of pay from 16 cents to 50 cents an hour ... Whenever a less skilled man can be slipped in at 18 cents, 18 and a half cents, 20 cents, 21 cents, 22 and a half cents, 24 cents, 25 cents and so on, a place is made for him and an occupation mapped out ... skill has become specialized to fit the anatomy' (158).

9 Kochan, Katz, and McKersie (1986) point out collective bargaining in many other industries, including those dominated by craft unions, operated in a more decentralized manner.

10 Seniority is not a principle. Justice and equity are principles; seniority is a procedure for translating principles into practice. ECWU local 800 uses seniority (to regulate lay-offs) and no hierarchy of job classes as procedures to sustain larger principles. Interestingly, a single job class of multi-skilled workers significantly increases the probability that lay-offs would in fact be carried out by seniority – something not always possible in traditionally designed plants.

11 As Johansson (1986) points out, Taylor was also interested in blunting the emerging political consciousness of unskilled workers.

Chapter 2

1 Often unions view work redesign as a necessary concession in order to protect jobs rather than as a strategic opportunity to broaden their role in the workplace. Of course management attitudes play some part in shaping the unions' assessment.

2 For many Canadian unions the experience with work redesign has been negative. PSAC, for example, following several official experiments in the late 1970s changed its policy from one of support to rejection. One reason for this shift was the view that work redesign usually leads to changes in job classifications, an area in the federal public service which is outside the

scope of collective bargaining and therefore significant union influence. One PSAC component, the Union of National Defence Employees, continues to work with management in developing employee involvement programs at several Canadian Armed Forces bases.

3 It is interesting to note that in the original socio-technical studies of the Durham coal-mines in Britain (Trist and Bamforth 1951; Trist et al 1963) all the autonomous groups were based on a negotiated contract between the local unions and management which specified rights and responsibilities and the method of paying for the new way of working (Herbst 1985).

4 Multi-skilling means just what it says – the development of *skills* and not multi-tasking.

5 While the empirical evidence for Adler's claim is not clear-cut, the general trend does seem to be toward upskilling and reskilling. See, for example, *Connections for the Future: The Report of the Joint Human Resources Committee of the Canadian Electrical and Electronics Manufacturing Industry* (Toronto 1989).

Chapter 3

1 Economic pressure, however, does not mean economic determinism. As March and Simon (1958) have shown, managers seek a satisfying not an optimizing solution to problems of organization effectiveness.

2 I do not share the view of some social scientists (e.g., Child 1981) that a pluralist perspective necessarily assumes an approximate balance of power between conflicting interests and a consensus among these interests as the 'the rules of the game' or relies unduly on social psychology at the expense of other relevant disciplines.

Chapter 4

1 As Elden (1986) points out, conflict and co-operation are not necessarily opposite ends of a continuum. Organization can score both high and low on either dimension simultaneously.

2 The Kalmar case illustrates the concept of both organizational and technological choice. However, as Emery (1975) points out, the socio-technical design of the Kalmar factory retains some of the key principles of the assembly line.

Chapter 5

1 Similarly, Ed Cohen-Rosenthal (1987), assistant to the president of the International Union of Bricklayers and Allied Craftsmen, argues that:

'union meetings must change ... meetings need to be times not to ratify backroom decisions but to engage in serious dialogue with the membership and a real forum for decision making and education' (p 5).

2 With the notable exception of Hirschhorn (1988), the psychoanalytic foundation of sts thinking has been ignored in North America.

Chapter 6

1 One other property, the dominant form of conflict resolution, appears in the chemical plant list but not in the literature. However, as explained in chapter 4, this property is highlighted in the literature but not identified as a formal property.

2 Trist (1981) argues that western society is weak in the middle: 'Too little effective social structuring is available between institutions concerned with the management of the overall aggregate and the single organization' (p 54). Two promising middle-level union management initiatives in Canada are the Joint Human Resources Committee of the Electrical and Electronics Industry and the Canadian Steel Trades and Employment Congress. Even the UE, for a time, was actively involved in the former. In the United States, geographically based rather than sector-based labor management committees appear to be the preferred form of 'mid-level' innovation.

3 For an interesting discussion of the changing nature of skill in the pulp and paper industry, see S. Zuboff, 'Technologies That Informate: Implications for Human Resource Management in the Computerized Industrial Workplace,' in Lawrence and Walton (1985).

Bibliography

Abernathy, W., K. Clark, and A. Kantrow. 1981. 'The New Industrial Competition.' *Harvard Business Review* 59: 68–81
– 1983. *Industrial Renaissance*. New York: Basic Books
Ackoff, R. 1973. 'Planning in the Systems Age.' *Indian Journal of Statistics*, series b, vol. 35 (2): 149–64
Ackoff, Russell, and F.E. Emery. 1972. *On Purposeful Systems*. New York: Aldine
Adams, G. 1981. 'Industrial Democracy: A Canadian Perspective.' Paper presented to the Canadian Institute of Advanced Legal Studies, Cambridge, England, 31 July
Adler, P.S. 1986. 'New Technologies, New Skills.' *California Management Review* 9 (1): 9–28
Aguren, S., C. Bredbacka, R. Hansson, K. Ihrgren, and K. Karlsson. 1984. *Volvo Kalmar Revisited*. Stockholm: Efficiency and Participation Development Council, SAF, LO, PTK
Aguren, S., R. Hansson, and K.G. Karlsson. 1976. *The Volvo Kalmar Plant*. The Rationalization Council, SAF-LO, Stockholm
Aitken, H.G.S. 1960. *Taylorism at Watertown Arsenal*. Cambridge, Mass.: Harvard University Press
Argyris, C. 1962. *Interpersonal Competence and Organizational Effectiveness*. Homewood, Ill.: Dorsey Press
Argyris, Chris, and Donald A. Schon. 1974. *Theory in Practice: Increasing Professional Effectiveness*. San Francisco: Jossey-Bass
Argyris, C., and D.A. Schon. 1978. *Organizational Learning: A Theory of Action Perspective*. London: Addison-Wesley
Arthurs, H. 1966. 'Challenge and Response in the Law of Labour Relations.' In J. Crispo. ed., *Industrial Relations: Challenges and Responses*. Toronto: University of Toronto Press

174 / Bibliography

Auberts, V. 1963. 'Competition and Dissensus: Two Types of Conflict and of Conflict Resolution.' *Journal of Conflict Resolution* 7: 26–7

Bacharach, S.B., and E.J. Lawler. 1980. *Power and Politics in Organizations*. San Francisco: Jossey-Bass

– 1981. *Bargaining*. San Francisco: Jossey-Bass

Barbash, J. 1964. 'The Elements of Industrial Relations.' *British Journal of Industrial Relations* 2: 66–78

– 1977. 'Unions Advance Quality of Work through Collective Bargaining.' *World Work Review* 21 (March): 31

Barko, W., and W. Pasmore. 1986. 'Introductory Statement to the Special Issue on Sociotechnical Systems: Innovations in Designing High Performing Systems.' *Journal of Applied Behavioural Science* 22 (3): 195–9

Batstone, E., I. Boraston, and S. Frenkel. 1978. *Shop Stewards in Action*. Oxford: Basil Blackwell

Batt, W.L., and E. Weinberg. 1978. 'Labour-Management Co-operation Today.' *Harvard Business Review* 59: 96–104

Bazerman, M.H., and R.J. Lewicki. 1985. 'Contemporary Research Directions in the Study of Negotiations in Organizations: A Selective Overview: *Occupational Behaviour* 6: 1–17

Beatty, D. 1984. 'The Role of the Arbitrator: A Liberal Version.' *University of Toronto Law Journal* 34 (2): 136–9

Berner, B. 1986. 'Sociology, Technology and Work.' In U. Himmelstrand, ed., *The Social Reproduction of Organizations and Culture*. London: Sage Publications

Blackler, R., and C. Brown. 1975. 'The Impending Crisis in Job Design.' *The Journal of Occupational Psychology* 48: 185–93

Blake, R., and J. Mouton. 1979. 'Intergroup Problem Solving Organization: From Theory to Practice.' In W. Austin and S. Warchel, eds., *The Social Psychology of Intergroup Relations*. Monterey: Brooks

Bluestone, I. 1977. 'Creating a New World of Work.' *International Labour Review* 115: 1–10

– 1982. 'Workers Have Brains Too.' *Workplace Democracy* 9: 4

Bradley, K., and S. Hill. 1983. 'After Japan. The Quality Circle Transplant and Productive Efficiency.' *British Journal of Industrial Relations* 9 (3): 291–311

Brossard, M. 1981. 'North American Unions and Semi-Autonomous Work Group.' In *Quality of Working Life: The Canadian Scene* vol 4 (1): 1–5. Ottawa: Labour Canada

Brown, L.D., and J.C. Brown. 1983. 'Organizational Microcosms and Ideological Negotiation.' In M. Bazerman and R. Lewicki, eds., *Negotiating in Organizations*. London: Sage Publications

Brunet, L. 1981. 'Quality Circles: Can They Improve QWL?' In *Quality of*

Working Life: The Canadian Scene vol 4 (2): 1–2. Ottawa: Labour Canada

Buroway, M. 1979. *Manufacturing Consent: Changes in the Labour Process under Monopoly Capitalism*. Chicago: University of Chicago Press

Camens, S. 1983. 'Steel: An Industry at the Crossroads.' *Productivity Brief*. Houston: American Productivity Center

Chamberlain, N., and J. Kuhn. 1965. *Collective Bargaining*. New York: McGraw-Hill

Chamberlain, N.W. 1945. *The Union Challenge to Management Control*. New York: Harper

Cherns, A.B. 1976. 'The Principles of Organizational Design.' *Human Relations* 29 (8): 783–92

Child, J. 1981. 'Comment.' In A. Thompson and M. Warner, eds., *Behavioural Sciences and Industrial Relations: Some Problems of Integration*. Guildford: Gower

Chinoy, E. 1965. *Automobile Workers and the American Dream*. Boston: Beacon Press

Cirourel, A. 1973. *Cognitive Sociology*. Free Press

Clegg, C.W. 1984. 'The Derivation of Job Designs.' *Journal of Occupational Behaviour*, vol. 5 (2): 131–46

Cohen, S., and J. Zysman. 1987. *Manufacturing Matters: The Myth of the Post-Industrial Society*. New York: Basic Books

Cohen-Rosenthal, E. 1984. 'The Other Side of the Coin: The Impact of QWL. Programs on the Union as an Organization.' *Labor Studies* 8 (3) 229–43

– 1987. 'A New Age for Unions.' Paper presented to the Einar Thorsrud Memorial Symposium and Workshop, Oslo, 13–16 June

Cole, R.E. 1979. *Work Mobility and Participation*. Berkely: University of California Press

Committee on the Effective Implementation of Advanced Manufacturing Technology. 1987. *Human Resource Practices for Implementing Advanced Manufacturing*. Washington: National Academy Press

Commons, J.R. 1934. *Institutional Economics: Its Place in the Political Economy*. New York: Macmillan

– ed., 1921, *Trade Unions and Labor Problems*. Boston: Ginn and Company

Crozier, M. 1964. *The Bureaucratic Phenomenon*. London: Tavistock

Crozier, M., and E. Freidberg. 1980. *Actions and Systems*. Chicago: University of Chicago Press

Dalton, M. 1959. *Men Who Manage*. New York: Wiley

Davis, L. 1980. 'Individuals and the Organization.' *California Management Review* 22 (2): 5–14

– 1977. 'Evoluting Alternative Organization Designs: Their Sociotechnical Bases.' *Human Relations* 39 (3): 361–73

– 1983. 'Workers and Technology: The Necessary Joint Basis for Organizational Effectiveness.' *National Productivity Review*, Winter, 7–14

Davis, L.E., and C.S. Sullivan. 1980. 'A Labor Management Contract and Quality of Working Life.' *Occupational Behavior*, vol. 1: 29–41

Davis, L.E., and J.C. Taylor. 1975. 'Technology Effects on Jobs, Work and Organizational Structure: A Contingency View.' In L.E. Davis and A.B. Cherns, eds., *Quality of Working Life: Problems, Prospects and State of the Art*. New York: Free Press

Deutsch, M. 1973. *The Resolution of Conflict*. New Haven: Yale University Press

Diesing, Paul. 1971. *Patterns of Discovery in Social Sciences*. Chicago: Aldine-Atherton

Docquier, G. 1982. 'Work in Canada; Crisis and Opportunity.' Speech to the Canadian Council of Working Life Conference, 1 November

Doeringer, P. and M. Piore. 1971. *Internal Labour Markets*. Lexington: D.C. Heath and Co

Dunlop, J.T. 1958. *Industrial Relations Systems*. New York: Holt

Eccles, R. 1983. 'Negotiations in the Organizational Environment: A Framework for Discussion.' In M.H. Bazerman and R.J. Lewicki, eds., *Negotiating in Organizations*. Beverly Hills: Sage Publications

Economic Council of Canada. 1987. *Making Technology Work*. Ottawa: Supply and Services Canada

Edwards, R. 1979. *Contested Terrain: The Transformation of the Workplace in the Twentieth Century*. New York: Basic Books

Ehn, P. 1988. *Work-Oriented Design of Computer Artifacts*. Stockholm: Arbetslivscentrum

Elden, M. 1986. 'Sociotechnical Systems Ideas as Public Policy in Norway: Empowering Participation through Worker-Managed Change.' *Journal of Applied Behavioural Science* 22 (3): 239–56

Elden, M., V. Haun, M. Lewin, T. Nilssen, B. Rasmussen, and K. Veium. 1982. *Good Technology Is Not Enough*. Trondheim: IFIM

Emery, F.E. 1959a. *Systems Thinking*. Baltimore: Penguin

– 1959b. 'Characteristics of Sociotechnical Systems.' Tavistock Institute Paper TIHR 527, London

– 1963. 'The Case Study Method.' Document T265. London: Tavistock

– 1974. 'Participant Design.' Canberra: Centre of Continuing Education, ANU

– 1975. 'The Assembly Line – Its Logic and Our Future.' Occasional Paper No. 7, Australian National University, Canberra

– 1977. *Futures We Are In*. Leiden: Martinus Nijhoff

– 1978. *The Emergence of a New Paradigm of Work*. Canberra: Centre for Continuing Education, ANU

– 1980. 'Designing Socio-technical Systems for "Green Field Sites." ' *Occupational Behavior* 1: 19–27

Emery, F.E., and E. Thorsrud. 1976. *Democracy at Work*. Leiden: Martinus Nijhoff

Emery, F.E., and E.L. Trist 1964. 'The Causal Texture of Organizational Environments.' *Human Relations* 188: 21–32

– 1973. *Towards a Social Ecology*. New York: Plenum

Extra, J. 1982. 'Book Reviews.' *European Journal of Social Psychology* 12: 4

Ford, R.N. 1969. *Motivation through the Work Itself*. New York: American Management Association

Forrest, A. 1978. *Unions and the Collective Bargaining Process*. Toronto: OISE

Foucault, M. 1972. *The Archaeology of Knowledge and the Discourse of Language*. New York: Pantheon

French, J.R.P., and B. Raven. 1959. 'The Bases of Social Power.' In D. Cartwright, ed., *Studies in Social Power*. Ann Arbor, Mich.: University of Michigan

Galbraith, J. 1973. *Designing Complex Organizations*. Reading, Mass.: Addison-Wesley

– 1977. *Organization Design*. Reading, Mass.: Addison-Wesley

Galbraith, J.R., and D.A. Nathanson. 1978. *Strategy Implementation: The Role of Structure and Process*. New York: West

Galbraith, K. 1967. *The New Industrial State*. New York: Houghton Mifflin

Gardell, B. 1983. 'Worker Participation and Autonomy: A Multi-level Approach to Democracy at the Work Place.' In C. Crouch and F. Heller, eds., *Organizational Democracy and Political Processes*. New York: J. Wiley and Sons Ltd

Gershenfeld, W.J., and S.M. Schmidt. 1982. 'Structure and Administration of Large Local Unions.' A Report to the US Department of Labor

Gersuny, C. 1982. 'Origins of Seniority Provisions in Collective Bargaining.' *Labor Law* 33: 8

Gilmore, T.H. 1982. 'Leadership and Boundary Management.' *Journal of Applied Behavioral Science* 18 (3): 343–56

Glaser, B.G., and A.L. Strauss. 1967. *The Discovery of Grounded Theory*. Chicago: Aldine

Goldberg, A. 1973. Cited in P. Prasow, 'The Theory of Management Reserved Rights Revisited.' In G. Somers, ed., *Industrial Relations Research Association Series, Proceedings of the 26th Annual Winter Meeting*, December, 75–6

Goodman, P., and J. Dean. 1981. 'Why Productivity Efforts Fail.' Paper presented at the American Psychological Association, Los Angeles, and the QWL and 80s Conference, Toronto

Griffin, L., M. Wallace, and B. Rubin. 1986. 'Capitalism and Labor Organization.' *American Sociological Review* 51 (2): 147–75

Guillet, S. 1984. 'A Trade Union Agenda on Quality of Working Life' Paper presented to the Eurojobs Conference on Productivity and Quality of Working Life in an Age of Advanced Technology, Paris

Gulowsen, J. 1982. 'The Hearocracy.' Unpublished paper, Institute of Social Science, University of Tromso, Norway

Gustavsen, B. 1980: 'From Satisfaction to Collective Action: Trends in the Development of Research and Reform in Working Life.' *Economic and Industrial Democracy* 1 (2): 147–70

– 1981. 'Environmental Requirements and the Democratization of Industrial Organizations.' Unpublished paper

– 1983a. 'Automation and Work Organization: Policies and Practices in Market Economy Countries.' Working paper prepared for meeting of experts on automation, work organization, work intensity and occupational stress, International Labour Organization, Geneva

– 1983b. *Sociology as Action: On the Constitution of Alternative Realities*. Draft book manuscript. Oslo, Work Research Institutes

– 1986. 'Evolving Patterns of Enterprise Organization: The Move towards Greater Flexibility.' *International Labour Review* 125 (4): 307–81

– 1987. Organization Development within the LOM Programme.' Draft Working Paper, Arbetslivscentrum, Stockholm

Gustavsen, Bjorn, and P. Engelstad. 1986. 'The Design of Conference and the Evolving Role of Democratic Dialogue in Changing Working Life.' *Human Relations* 39 (2): 101–16

Gustavsen, B., and G. Hunnius. 1981. *New Patterns of Work Reform*. Oslo: Universitetsforlaget

Gyllenhammar, P. 1977. *People at Work*. Reading, Mass.: Addison-Wesley

Habermas, J. 1971. *Knowledge and Human Interest*. Boston: Beacon Press

Hackman, J., and E. Lawler. 1971. 'Employee Reactions to Job Characteristics.' *Journal of Applied Psychology* Monograph 55: 259–86

Hackman, J.R., G.R. Oldham, R. Jansen, and K. Purdy. 1975. 'A New Strategy for Job Enrichment.' *California Management Review*, Summer, 57–71

Halpern, N. 1983. 'Strategies for Dealing with Forces Acting on the Process of Organization Change in a Unionized Setting: A Case Study.' EdD dissertation, University of Toronto

– 1984. 'Socio-technical Systems Design: The Shell Sarnia Experience.' In J.B. Cunningham, and T.H. White eds., *Quality of Working Life, Contemporary Cases* Ottawa: Labour Canada

Heckscher, C. 1980. 'Worker Participation and Management Control.' *Journal of Social Reconstruction* 77–102

– 1981. 'Democracy at Work: In Whose Interests? The Politics of Worker Participation.' PhD dissertation, Harvard University

– 1986. 'Multilateral Negotiation and the Future of American Labor.' *Negotiation Journal*, April: 140–54

– 1988. *The New Unionism*. New York: Basic Books

Herbst, D. 1985. 'Introduction to Socio-technical Thinking, a Dialogic Presentation.' Document Number 11/85, Work Research Institute, Oslo

Herbst, P. 1962. *Autonomous Group Functioning*. London: Tavistock

– 1974. *Sociotechnical Design*. London: Tavistock

– 1976. *Alternatives to Hierarchies*. Leiden: Martinus Nijhoff

Herding, R. 1972. *Job Control and Union Structure: A Study on Plant Level Conflict in the United States with a Comparative Perspective on West Germany*. Rotterdam: Rotterdam University Press

Hermand, E. 1966. *Determination of the Appropriate Bargaining Unit of Labour Relations Boards in Canada*. Ottawa: Canada Department of Labour

Heron, C. 1989. *The Canadian Labour Movement*. Toronto: James Lorimer

Herrick, N. 1985. 'Parallel Organizations in Unionized Settings: Implications for Organizational Research.' *Human Relations* 38 (10): 963–81

Herrick, N.Q., and M. MacCoby. 1975. 'Humanizing Work: A Priority Goal of the 1970's.' In L.E. Davis and A.B. Cherns, eds., *The Quality of Working Life*, vol. 1. New York: Free Press

Herzberg, F., B. Mausner, and B. Snyderman. 1959. *The Motivation of Work*. New York: Wiley

Hill, C.P. 1971. *Towards a New Philosophy of Management*. London: Gower Press

Hirschhorn, L. 1982. 'The Soul of a New Worker.' *Working Papers Magazine* 9 (1, Jan–Feb): 42–7

– 1984. *Beyond Mechanization*. Cambridge, Mass.: MIT Press

– 1988. *The Workplace Within*. Cambridge, Mass.: MIT Press

Hoxie, R. 1966. *Scientific Management and Labor*. Reprint of 1915 edition. New York: Kelley

Hyman, R. 1981. *Industrial Relations: A Marxist Introduction*. London: Macmillan

Jacoby, S. 1983. 'Union Management Corporation in the United States: Lessons from the 1920's.' *Industrial and Labor Relations Review* 37 (1, October): 18–33

– 1984. 'The Development of Internal Labor Markets in American Manufacturing Firms.' In P. Osterman, ed., *Internal Labor Markets*. Cambridge, Mass.: MIT Press

Jain, H.C., and M. Ohtsu. 1983. 'Viability of Japanese Industrial Relations System in the Canadian Context.' Canadian Industrial Relations Association, 20th Annual Meeting, Ottawa, 1–3 June

Jaques, E. 1955.'Social Systems as Defence against Persecutory and Depressive Anxiety.' In *New Directions in Psycho-analysis*. London: Tavistock

Jeans, J.S. 1902. *American Industrial Conditions and Industrial Competition*. London: The British Iron Trade Association

Johansson, A. 1986. 'The Labour Movement and the Emergence of Taylorism.' *Economic and Industrial Democracy* 7: 449–85

Kanter, R.M. 1978. 'Work in America.' *Daedalus* 107: 53–4

Kaplan, A. 1964. *The Conduct of Inquiry*. San Francisco: Chandler

Katz, H.C. 1984. 'The U.S. Automobile Collective Bargaining System in Transition.' *British Journal of Industrial Relations* 22 (2 July): 205–17

– 1985. *Shifting Gears*. Cambridge, Mass.: MIT Press

Kelly, J.E. 1978. 'A Reappraisal of Sociotechnical Systems Theory.' *Human Relations* 31 (12): 1069–99

Kerr, C., J.T. Dunlop, F.H. Harbison, and C.A. Myers. 1960. *Industrialism and Industrial Man*. New York: Oxford University Press

Kerr, C., and L.H. Fisher. 1957. 'Plant Sociology: The Elites and the Aborigines.' In M. Komarovsky, ed., *Common Frontiers of Social Sciences*. New York: Free Press

Kets de Vries, F.R. 1976. 'On Power: Toward a Protean Perspective.' Faculty of Management Working Paper, McGill University, Montreal

Klein, J.A. 1984. 'Why Supervisors Resist Employee Involvement.' *Harvard Business Review*, Sept–Oct: 87–95

Kochan, T. 1988. 'On the Human Side of Technology.' *ICL Technical Journal*, November: 391–400

Kochan, T., and T. Jick. 1978. 'The Public Sector Mediation Process: A Theory and Empirical Examination.' *Conflict Resolution* 22: 209–40

Kochan, T., H. Katz, and R. McKersie. 1986. *The Transformation of American Industrial Relations*. New York: Basic Books

Kochan, T., H. Katz, and N. Mower. 1984. *Worker Participation and American Unions: Threat of Opportunity?* Kalamazoo: W.E. Upjohn Institute for Employment Research

Kochan, T., and M. Piore. 1984. 'Will the New Industrial Relations Last? Implications for the American Labor Movement.' *Annals of the American Academy of Political and Social Science*, May: 177–89

Kochan, T., and A. Verma. 1983. 'Negotiating in Organizations: Blending Industrial Relations and Organizational Behavior Approaches.' In M.H. Baserman, and R.J. Lewicki, eds., *Negotiating in Organizations*. Beverly Hills: Sage Publications

Kochan, T.A., and H.C. Katz. 1983. 'Collective Bargaining, Work, Organization and Worker Participation: The Return to Plant Level Bargaining.' *Labor Law Journal* 34: 524–30

Kuhn, J. 1962. *Bargaining in Grievance Settlement: The Power of the Industrial Workgroups*. New York: Columbia University Press

Kuhn, T.S.C. 1970. *The Structure of Scientific Revolutions*. Chicago: University of Chicago Press

Kumar, P. 1972. 'Differentials in Wage Rates of Unskilled Labor in Canadian

Manufacturing Industries.' *Industrial and Labor Relations Review* 26 (1, October): 643–4

Laberge, R. 1978. 'Canadians and the Work Ethic.' *Labour Gazette* 21–6. Special edition, 'Adapting to a Changing World,' George F. Sanderson, ed. Ottawa: Labour Canada

Lawler, E. 1978. 'The New Plant Revolution.' *Organizational Dynamics*, Winter: 3–12

Lawler, E., and S. Mohrman. 1985. 'Quality Circles after the Fad.' *Harvard Business Review*, Jan–Feb: 65–71

Lawrence, P. 1985. 'History of Human Resource Management in American Industry.' In P. Lawrence, and R. Walton, eds., *H.R.M.: Trends and Changes*. Cambridge, Mass.: Harvard Business School

Lawrence, P., and R. Walton, eds. 1985. *H.R.M.: Trends and Changes*. Cambridge, Mass.: Harvard Business School

Lawrence, W.G. 1982. 'Some Psychic and Political Dimensions of Work Experiences.' Occasional Paper No. 2. London: Tavistock

Leavitt, H.J. 1978. 'Some Effects of Certain Communication Patterns on Group Performance.' In D. Pugh, ed., *Organizational Theory*. Baltimore: Penguin

Lemelin, M. 1981. 'Trade Unions and Work Organization Experiments.' In *Adapting to a Changing World* II. 110–20. Ottawa: Labour Canada

Lewin, D. 1981. 'Collective Bargaining and the Quality of Work Life.' *Organizational Dynamics*, Autumn, 37–53

Lichtenstein, N. 1982. 'Industrial Democracy, Contract Unionism and the National War Labor Board.' *Labor Law*, August: 524–31

Lie, M. 1983. 'The Significant of Technology for Women's Work.' Working Paper from the Research Programme Technology and Women's Work.' IFTM, University of Trondheim

Lijphart, A. 1971. 'Comparative Politics and the Comparative Method.' *American Political Science Review* 65: 682–93

Likert, R. 1967. *The Human Organization*. New York: McGraw-Hill

Lipset, S.M., M.A. Trow, and J.S. Coleman. 1956. *Union Democracy: The Internal Politics of the International Typographical Union*. Glencoe, Ill.: Free Press

List, W. 1985. 'Study Sees Era of Decline for Unions.' *Globe and Mail*, Toronto, 11 March, B9

Lodge, G.C. 1975. *The New American Ideology*. New York: A.A. Knopf

Lysgaard, S. 1971. *Arbeiderkollektivet* (The Worker Collective). Oslo: Universitetsforaget

Macy, B. 1980. 'The Bolivar Quality of Working Life Program: A Longitudinal Behavioral and Performance Assessment.' Proceedings of the 32nd Annual Meeting of the Industrial Relations Research Association, Madison, Wisc.

Mallet, S. 1963. *La Nouvelle Classe Ouvrière*. Paris: Editions du Seuil

Mansell, J. 1980. 'Dealing with Some Obstacles to Innovation in the Work Place.' Issues in the Quality of Working Life: A Series of Occasional Paper, 1. Toronto: Ontario Quality of Working Life Centre
– 1983. 'The Next Five Years.' Internal Document. Toronto: Ontario Quality of Working Life Centre
– 1987a. *Workplace Innovation in Canada*. Economic Council of Canada. Ottawa: Supply and Services Canada
– 1987b. 'Changes in Work Organization and the role of Unions, the Canadian Experience.' Paper presented to the PTK seminar, Unions in the 1990's, 225–7, May, Stockholm
Mansell, J., and T. Rankin. 1983. 'Changing Organizations: The Quality of Working Life Process.' Issues in the Quality of Working Life: A Series of Occasional Papers, 4. Toronto: Ontario Quality of Working Life Centre
March, J., and H. Simon. 1958. *Organizations*. New York: Wiley
Marginson, P. 1984. 'The Distinctive Effects of Plant and Company Size on Workplace Industrial Relations.' *British Journal of Industrial Relations* 2 (1): 1–14
Mason, R. 1982. *Participatory and Workplace Democracy*. Carbondale: Southern Illinois University Press
Mayo, E. 1946. *The Human Problem of an Industrial Civilization*. Cambridge, Mass.: Harvard University Press
Menzies, I.E.P. 1960. 'A Case Study in the Functioning of Social Systems as a Defence against Anxiety.' *Human Relations* 13: 95–121
Merkle, J. 1980. *Management and Ideology*. Berkeley: University of California Press
Michels, R. 1962. *Political Parties*. New York: Free Press
Miller, E.J. 1959. 'Territory, Technology and Time: The Internal Differentiation of Complex Production Systems.' *Human Relations* 22: 3
Montgomery, M. 1966. *A Union Primer on Contract Negotiations: A Guide to the Collective Bargaining Process*. Toronto: USWA
Morgan, G. 1986. *Images of Organization*. London: Sage
Morgan, G., and R. Ramirez. 1984. 'Action Learning: A Holographic Metaphor for Guiding Social Change.' *Human Relations* 37 (1): 1–10
Morgan, G., and L. Smircich. 1980. 'The Case for Qualitative Research.' *Academy of Management Review* 5: 491–500
Mulder, M. 1971. 'Power Equalization through Participation.' *Administrative Science Quarterly* 16: 31–9
– 1977. *The Daily Power Game*. Leiden: Martinus Nijhoff
Murray, P. 1940. *Organized Labor and Production*.
Myers, S. 1970. *Every Employee a Manager*. New York: McGraw-Hill
Nadworny, M.J. 1955. *Scientific Management and the Unions*. Cambridge, Mass.: Harvard University Press

Nash, A. 1983. *The Union Steward: Duties, Rights and Status*. Ithaca: New York School of Industrial and Labor Relations

Nicholson, N. 1976. 'The role of the Shop Steward: An Empirical Case Study.' *Industrial Relations Journal* 7 (1): 15–26

Nightingale, D. 1982. *Workplace Democracy*. Toronto: University of Toronto Press

OECD. 1986. 'The Evolution of New Technology, Work and Skills in the Service Sector.' Centre for Educational Research and Innovation. Paris

Olsen, D. 1981. 'Labor's Stake in a Democratic Workplace.' *Working Papers for a New Society* vol. 8: 2

Olsen, M. *The Logic of Collective Action: Public Goods and the Theory of Groups*. Cambridge, Mass.: Harvard University Press

Ondrack, D., and M. Evans. 1980. 'The Shell Chemical Plant at Sarnia (Canada): An Example of Union-Management Collaboration.' In H. Jain, ed., *Worker Participation*, 257–74. New York: Praeger

Osterman, P. 1984. *Internal Labour Markets*. Cambridge, Mass.: MIT Press

Ouchi, W.G. 1977. 'The Relationship between Organizational Structure and Organizational Control.' *Administrative Science Quarterly* 22: 95–113

Parker, M. 1985. *Inside the Circle*. Boston: South End Press

Parker, M., and J. Slaughter. 1988. *Choosing Sides: Unions and the Team Concept*. Boston: South End Press

Pasmore, W. 1988. *Designing Effective Organizations*. Toronto: Wiley

Pasmore, W., C. Francis, I. Haldeman, and A. Shani. 1982. 'Social-Technical Systems: A North American Reflection on Empirical Studies of the Seventies.' *Human Relations* 35 (12): 1179–1204

Pateman, C. 1970. *Participation and Democratic Theory*. Cambridge, England: University of Cambridge Press

– 1982. Introduction in R. Mason, *Participatory and Workplace Democracy*. Carbondale: Southern Illinois University Press

Pava, C. 1979. 'State of the Art in American Autonomous Work Group Design.' Unpublished paper, Philadelphia: University of Pennsylvania, Management and Behavioral Science Center, Wharton School

– 1980. 'Towards a Concept of Normative Incrementalism.' PhD dissertation, University of Pennsylvania

– 1981. 'Microprocessor Technology and the Quality of Working Life.' A Report to the Ontario Quality of Working Life Centre, Toronto

– 1983. *Managing New Office Technology: An Organizational Strategy*. New York: Free Press

– 1986. 'Redesigning Sociotechnical Systems Design: Concepts and Methods for the 1990's.' *Journal of Applied Behavioural Science* 22 (3): 201–21

Perlman, S. 1928. *A Theory of the Labor Movement*. New York: A.M. Kelley

Piore, M. 1982. 'American Labor and the Industrial Crisis.' *Challenge* 25 (2): 5–11

Piore, M., and C.F. Sabel. 1984. *The Second Industrial Divide*. New York: Basic Books

Polanyi, M. 1962. *Personal Knowledge*. London: Routledge and Kegan Paul

Poza, E. 1980. 'Success Story: The Team Approach to Work Restructuring.' *Organization Dynamics* 8 (3): 3–25

Poza, E.J. 1983. 'Twelve Actions to Build Strong U.S. Factories.' *Sloan Management Review*, Fall, 27–38

Pruitt, D.G. 1983. 'Achieving Integrative Agreements.' In M.H. Baserman and R.J. Lewicki, eds., *Negotiating in Organizations*. Beverly Hills: Sage Publications

Pruitt, D.G., and P. Carnevale, 1982. 'Threat Capacity and the Choice between Independence and Interdependence.' *Personality and Social Psychology* 4: 252–5

Rankin, T., and J. Mansell. 1986. 'Integrating Collective Bargaining and New Forms of Work Organization.' *National Productivity Review*, Autumn, 338–47

Reich, R. 1983. *The Next American Frontier*. New York: Times Books

– 1987. 'The Team as a Hero.' *Harvard Business Review*, May–June: 77–83

Reimer, N. 1979. 'Oil, Chemical and Atomic Workers International Union and the Quality of Working Life – A Union Perspective.' *Quality of Working Life: The Canadian Scene*, Winter, 5–7

– 1980. In *QWL FOCUS: The Newsjournal of the Ontario Quality of Working Life Centre*. Ontario Ministry of Labour. Vol. 4 (1, Spring): 20

Reynaud, D. 1983. 'Change in Collective Identities.' In C. Crouch and F. Heller, eds., *Organizational Democracy and Political Processes*. New York: John Wiley and Sons, Ltd

Rice, A.K. 1958. *Productivity and Social Organization: The Ahmedabad Experiment*. London: Tavistock

Roberts, R. 1978. 'Labour Reform: Studies in the Toronto Union Movement, 1890–1914.' Phd Dissertation, University of Toronto

– 1984. 'Lots of Um's: Collective Bargaining and Industrial Democracy.' Unpublished paper, Ontario Quality of Working Life Centre, Toronto

Ronchi, D., and W. Morgan. 1980. 'Persisting and Prevailing in Springfield, Ohio.' Paper presented at the QWL and the 80's. An International Conference, 31 August–4 September, Toronto

Rosenbrock, H.H. 1983. 'Robots and People.' *Work and People* 9 (2): 14–18

Salaman, 1981. *Class and the Corporation*. Glasgow: Fontana

Sandberg, A. 1986. *Trade Union Strategies in Production Issues: Some Swedish Experiences*. Stockholm: Swedish Centre for Working Life

Sandberg, T. 1982. *Work Organization and Autonomous Groups*. Stockholm: Liberforlag

Sayles, L.R., and G. Strauss. 1953. *The Local Union: Its Place in the Industrial Plant*. New York: Harper and Row

Schein, E.H. 1969. *Process Consultation: Its Role in Organization Development*. Reading, Mass.: Addison-Wesley

Schlesinger, L.A., and R. Walton. 1977. 'The Process of Work Restructuring and Its Impact on Collective Bargaining.' *Monthly Labor Review* 100 (4): 52–5

Schneider, L. 1985. 'Worker Participation in Technological Change: Interests, Influence and Scope.' Unpublished paper, Kennedy School of Government, Harvard University

Schon, D. 1971. *Beyond the Stable State*. New York: Basic Books

Selznick, P. 1957. *Leadership in Administration*. New York: Harper and Row

Shwayder, D.S. 1965. *The Stratification of Behaviour*. London: Routledge and Kegan Paul

Silverman, D. 1971. *The Theory of Organizations: A Sociotechnical Framework*. New York: Basic Books

Slichter, S. 1941. *Union Policies and Industrial Management*. Washington: Brookings Institute

Steelworker. July 1955. Cited in A. Forrest. 'The Co-operative Wage Study.' Unpublished manuscript

Stein, B.A., and R.M. Kanter. 1980. 'Building the Parallel Organization: Creating Mechanisms for Permanent Quality at Worklife.' *Applied Behavioral Science* 16: 371–88

Stevenson, W.B., J.L. Pearce, and L.W. Porter. 1985. 'The Concept of "Coalition" in Organization Theory and Research.' *Academy of Management Review* 10 (2): 256–68

Stinson, J. 1982. 'The QWL Delusion.' *CUPE Facts*, June–July, 14–16

Stone, K. 1975. 'The Origins of Job Structure in the Steel Industry.' In D. Gordon, ed., *Labour Market Segmentation*. Lexington: Heath

Strauss, A. 1978. *Negotiations*. San Francisco: Jossey-Bass

Strauss, G. 1977. 'Managerial Practices.' In J.R. Hackman, and J.L. Suttle, eds., *Improving Life at Work*. Santa Monica, Calif.: Goodyear

Susman, G. 1976. *Autonomy at work*. New York: Praeger

– 1983. 'Action Research: A Sociotechnical Systems Perspective.' In G. Morgan, ed., *Beyond Method: Strategies for Social Research*. Beverly Hills: Sage

– 1986. 'A Sociotechnical Analysis of the Integrated Factory.' *Journal of Applied Behavioural Science* 22 (3): 257–70

Taylor, F.E. 1911. *The Principles of Scientific Management*. New York: Harper and Bros

Taylor, J. 1971. 'Some Effects of Technology in Organizational Change.' *Human Relations* 24: 105–23

Tchobanian, R. 1975. 'Trade Unions and Humanization at Work.' *International Labour Review* 3: 199–217

Thompson, J. 1967. *Organizations in Action.* New York: McGraw-Hill

Trist, E.L. 1976. 'A Concept of Organizational Ecology.' *Australian Journal of Management* 2 (2): 162–175

– 1981. 'The Evolution of Socio-technical Systems.' In A. Van de Ven and W. Joyce, ed., *Perspectives on Organization Design and Behaviour*. New York: Wiley Interscience

– 1983. 'QWL and the 80's.' In H. Kolodny and H. Van Beinum, eds., *The Quality of Working Life and the 1980's*. New York: Praeger

Trist, E., and K. Bamforth. 1951. 'Some Social and Psychological Consequences of the Long Wall Method of Goal Getting.' *Human Relations* 4 (1): 3–38

Trist, E.L., G.W. Higgin, H. Murray, and A.B. Pollock. 1963. *Organizational Choice: The Loss, Rediscovery and Transformation of a Work Tradition.* London: Tavistock

Trist, E.L., G.L. Susman, and G.R. Brown. 1977. 'An Experiment in Autonomous Working in an American Underground Coal Mine.' *Human Relations* 30 (3): 201–36

UE. 1984. *Quality Circles.* Resolution adopted by the 46th Convention of the United Electrical, Radio and Machine Workers of America

Ulman, L. 1974. 'Connective Bargaining and Competitive Bargaining.' *Scottish Journal of Political Economy* 21 (2): 97–109

United States National Research Council. 1986. *Human Resources Practices for Implementing Advanced Manufacturing Technology.* Washington, DC: National Academy Press

Van Beinum, H. 1984. 'Coming to Terms with QWL.' Unpublished paper, Ontario Quality of Working Life Centre, Toronto

– 1985. 'On the Meaning of QWL.' Unpublished manuscript, Ontario Quality of Working Life Centre, Toronto

Van de Ven, A.H., and M.A. Morgan. 1980. 'A Revised Framework for Organizational Assessment.' In E. Lawlor, D. Nadler, and C. Cammen, eds., *Organizational Assessment*. New York: Wiley

Van Maanen, J. 1979. 'Reclaiming Qualitative Methods for Organizational Research.' *Administrative Science Quarterly* 24: 520–6

Van Velzen, H. 1973. 'Coalitions and Network Analysis.' In J. Boissevain and J.C. Mitchell, eds., *Network Analysis Studies in Human Interaction*. Amsterdam: Mouton and Company

Vickers, Sir Geoffery. 1965. *The Art of Judgement.* London: Chapman and Hall

Von Otter, Casten. 1983. 'Facket och det post-industriella foretaget.' In *Vagval: Uppsatser om Nagra Demokrati-problem*. Stockholm: Brevskolan

Walsh, B. 1972. *The Name of the Game.* Sudbury: Mine Mill

Walton, R. 1975. 'The Diffusion of New Work Structures: Explaining Why Success Didn't Take.' *Organizational Dynamics*, Winter, 3–22
– 1984. 'From Control to Commitment: Transforming Work Force Management in the United States.' Paper prepared for the Harvard Business School's 75th Anniversary Colloquium on Technology and Productivity, 27–29 March
– 1980. 'Establishing and Maintaining High Commitment Work Systems.' In J. Kimberly and R. Miles, eds., *The Organizational Life Cycle*. New York: Jossey-Bass
Walton, R.E., and R.B. McKersie. 1965. *A Behavioral Theory of Labor Negotiations*. New York: McGraw-Hill
Warrian, P. 1980. 'A Union View of Quality of Working Life Issues in Resource Based Industries.' Paper presented at McGill University, Montreal, January
Watts, G. 1982. 'Management Incentives: Trick or Treat.' *Workplace Democracy* 9 (4, Summer): 1–2
Webb, E.J., D.T. Campbell, R.D. Schwartz, and L. Sechrest. 1966. *Unobtrusive Measures*. Chicago: Rand McNally
Weber, M. 1947. *The Theory of Social and Economic Organization*, trans. A. Henderson and T. Parsons. New York: Academic Press
Wells, D. 1987. *Empty Promises*. New York: Monthly Review Press
White, B. 1975. 'Union Response to the Humanization of Work: Explanatory Proposition.' *Human Resource Management*, Fall, 2–9
Williamson, O.E. 1963. 'A Model of Rational Managerial Behavior.' In C.M. Cyert and J.G. March, eds., *A Behavioral Theory of the Firm*. Englewood Cliffs: Prentice-Hall
Wittgenstein, L. 1961. *Tractatus Logico-Philosophicus*. London: Routledge and Kegan Paul
Wood, S. 1970. *The Degradation of Work?: Skill, Deskilling and the Braverman Debate*. London: Hutchinson
Woods, H.D. 1969. *Canadian Industrial Relations: A Report of the Task Force on Labour Relations*. Ottawa: Queen's Printer
Yin. R.K. 1981. 'The Case Study Crisis.' *Administrative Science Quarterly* 26: 58–65
Zartman, I.W. 1977. *The Negotiation Process*. London: Sage
Zuboff, S. 1982. 'New Worlds of Computer Mediated Work.' *Harvard Business Review* 60 (5): 145–52
– 1985. 'Technologies That Informate.' In P. Lawrence and R. Walton, eds., *H.R.M.: Trends and Changes*. Cambridge, Mass.: Harvard Business School

Index

Abernathy, W., K. Clark, and A. Kantrow, 4, 8, 24, 30
Adler, P., 54
Arthurs, H., 36
autonomous groups, 51–2

Bamforth, K., *see* Trist
Barko, W., and W. Pasmore, 9
Batstone, E., I. Boraston, and S. Frenkel, 122, 131
Bazerman, M., and R. Lewicki, 73, 75
Blackler, R., and C. Brown, 126
Bluestone, I., 42, 44
Boraston, I., *see* Batstone
Brown, C., *see* Blackler
Brown, G., *see* Trist

case study method, 61, 152
CAW, 42, 46, 151
Cherns, A., 6, 106
Clark, K., *see* Abernathy
craft unionism, 37–40, 154–9
Crozier, M., 21; and E. Freidberg, 141

Dalton, M., 113–15
Davis, Lou, 4, 6, 12, 54; and C.S. Sullivan, 5, 57, 109
Diesing, P., 65

Doeringer, P., and M. Piore, 18

ECWU local 800; collective action, 140–6; role of elected officials, 134–40; structure, 128–34
Ehn, P., 150
Elden, M., 141
Emery, Fred, xv, 4, 6, 7, 10, 11, 27, 33, 54, 55, 61, 114, 115; and E. Thorsrud, 7, 13, 141; and E. Trist, 4, 5, 6, 63, 96, 152
Engelstad, P., *see* Gustavsen

Freidberg, E., *see* Crozier
Frenkel, S., *see* Batstone

Galbraith, J., 45, 137
Galbraith, Kenneth, xii
Gardell, B., *see* Gustavsen
Gershenfeld, W., and S. Schmidt 130
Gilmore, T., 134, 142
Gustavsen, Björn, xiii, 4, 6, 9, 14, 16, 23, 24, 34, 47, 55, 141, 152; and P. Engelstad, 14; and B. Gardell, 141, 142

Halpern, N., 62, 66, 70
Heckscher, C., 4, 22, 24, 27, 37, 55, 155

Herbst, David, xv, 12, 15, 48, 51, 52, 53
Higgin, G., 8; *see also* Trist
Hirschhorn, Larry, 4, 12, 62, 155

indirect representation, 22–4
industrial unionism, 16–37

Jacoby, S., 4, 20
Jaques, E., 155
Japanese manufacturing, xi, 5
job control, 18–21
job enrichment, 48–9

Kantrow, A., *see* Abernathy
Katz, H., 18, 23, 45; *see also* Kochan
Kochan, Thomas, 8; and H. Katz, 20, 32, 56; and Katz and R. McKersie, 4, 14, 16, 23, 24, 29, 55, 63, 154; and Katz and N. Mower, 43, 47, 57; and M. Piore, 16, 18, 19; and A. Verma, 73, 74, 75, 140
Kuhn, T., 3

Lewicki, R., *see* Bazerman

Mansell, Jacquie, xii, 4, 29, 44, 49, 50, 54, 153; and T. Rankin, 53
McKersie, R.B., *see* Kochan *and* Walton
Menzies, I., 143–4
Morgan, G., 7
Mower, N., *see* Kochan
Murray, H., *see* Trist

negotiations theory, 72–5, 107–49
Nicholson, N., 137
Norwegian Industrial Democracy Project, xv

parallel systems, 49–51
Parker, M., 17; and J. Slaughter, 57

Pasmore, William, xiv, 6; *see also* Barko
Pateman, C., 23
Pava, C., 10, 30, 52, 53, 54, 55, 62, 73, 104, 105
Perlman, S., 19
Piore, M., 18; and C. Sabel, 4, 38, 63, 67, 155; *see also* Doeringer *and* Kochan
Pollock, A.B., *see* Trist
Pruitt, D., 101, 102

quality circles, 48, 49, 50, 51

Rankin, T., *see* Mansell
Reich, R., 11, 25, 62
Reimer, N., 42, 123, 124, 127
Rice, K., 8
Roberts, Wayne, 20, 24, 25, 26, 31, 32, 34, 35, 38
rules, 31–7

Sabel, C., *see* Piore
Sandberg, Åke, xii, 91, 150
Schmidt, S., *see* Gershenfeld
scientific management, 4
Selznick, P., 6
Shell chemical plant: background, 65–7; collective bargaining system, 76–115; organization design, 67–72
Slaughter, J., *see* Parker
socio-technical systems: design principles, 6–16; general, 4–6
solidarity, 24–8
Stone, K., 20, 38, 39, 40
Strauss, A., 113, 114, 115, 149
Sullivan, C.S., *see* Davis
Sullivan, S., 123
Susman, G., 6, 53, 54, 62; *see also* Trist

Taylor, Frederick, xii, 3, 26, 32, 37; design principles, 6–16; Taylorism, 3

Taylor, J., 54
technology, 53
Thorsrud, Einar, xv, 5; *see also* Emery
Trist, Eric, xv, 4, 5, 6, 7, 8, 41, 49,
    51, 52, 55, 62, 104, 109, 115; and
    K. Bamforth, 4; and G. Higgin,
    H. Murray, and A.B. Pollock, 115,
    154; and G. Susman, and G. Brown,
    46; *see also* Emery

UAW, 42, 46
unions: future, 149–51; and new forms
    of work organization, 41–8, 57–9

Van Beinum, H., 47
Verma, A., *see* Kochan
Von Otter, C., xii, 14

Walton, Richard, 4, 25, 44, 52, 55; and
    R.B. McKersie, 74, 84, 101, 104,
    112, 117, 118
Warrian, P., 21
Wells, D., 57
Woods, H.D., 36

Zuboff, S., 53

DATE DUE			
NOV 02 1998			